*"The secret is Christ in me,
not me in a different set of circumstances."*

Elisabeth Elliot

How a Wife Speaks

*Loving your husband well
through godly communication*

By Selena Frederick

LION PRESS

Published by Lion Press
a division of Vilicus LLC
2522 N. Proctor, PMB 461, Tacoma WA 98406
www.LionPress.org

How a Wife Speaks: Loving your husband well through godly communication, First Edition

Copyright © 2023 Selena Frederick

Printed in the United States of America

All rights reserved. No portion of this book may be reproduced, stored in a retrieval system, or transmitted in any form or by any means—electronic, mechanical, photocopy,recording, scanning, or other—except for brief quotations in critical reviews or articles, without the prior written permission of the publisher.

Unless otherwise noted, Scripture quotations are taken from the ESV® Bible (The Holy Bible, English Standard Version®). Copyright © 2001 by Crossway, a publishing ministry of Good News Publishers. Used by permission. All rights reserved.

Scripture quotations marked NIV are taken from the Holy Bible, New International Version®, NIV®. Copyright © 1973, 1978, 1984, 2011 by Biblica, Inc.® Used by permission of Zondervan. All rights reserved worldwide. www.zondervan.com. The "NIV" and "New International Version" are trademarks registered in the United States Patent and Trademark Office by Biblica, Inc.®

Scripture quotations marked NLT are taken from the Holy Bible, New Living Translation. Copyright © 1996, 2004, 2015 by Tyndale House Foundation. Used by permission of Tyndale House Ministries, Carol Stream, Illinois 60188. All rights reserved.

Scripture quotations marked NASB are taken from the New American Standard Bible® (NASB). Copyright © 1960, 1962, 1963, 1968, 1971, 1972, 1973, 1975, 1977, 1995, 2020 by The Lockman Foundation. Used by permission. www.Lockman.org

Scripture quotations marked CSB have been taken from the Christian Standard Bible®, Copyright © 2017 by Holman Bible Publishers. Used by permission. Christian Standard Bible® and CSB® are federally registered trademarks of Holman Bible Publishers.

Author portrait by Deb Hurlburt. Used by permission.

ISBN 978-0-9974713-7-3

Library of Congress Cataloging-in-Publication Data is forthcoming.

24 25 26 27 28   7 6 5 4 3 2

For Desiree,

"The wisest of women builds her house"

Let the words of my mouth
and the meditation of my heart
be acceptable in your sight,
O LORD, my rock and my redeemer.
Psalm 19:14

CONTENTS

Introduction.........................1

CHAPTER 1 Your Communication Garden............9
CHAPTER 2 The Words of an Excellent Wife...........21
CHAPTER 3 Off with the Old; On with the New........29
CHAPTER 4 Destroying Manipulation in Your Marriage..37
CHAPTER 5 The Wholehearted Yes..................49
CHAPTER 6 Respect is Not a Curse Word.............57
CHAPTER 7 The Words of a Wife to Her Beloved.......69
CHAPTER 8 To the Pen!..........................79
CHAPTER 9 Learning the Language of Gratitude........89
CHAPTER 10 Hangry and Tired?....................99
CHAPTER 11 The Truth About Lying.................107
CHAPTER 12 Tongue Taming......................119
CHAPTER 13 More Than A Meal....................127
CHAPTER 14 Communication Ruts and Tendencies.....135
CHAPTER 15 Hearing Everything He Never Said........141
CHAPTER 16 Consuming and Being Consumed........149
CHAPTER 17 Salty and Sweet, Oh What a Treat!........155
CHAPTER 18 A Soft Answer Turns Away Wrath.........165

Final Words........................173

INTRODUCTION

In the words of my sweet husband, "Good communication is the bulwark of every good marriage. And, sustained good communication is largely the responsibility of the husband—not *solely*, but largely." So where does that leave the wife who often feels like she is the primary communication initiator in the marriage? Or what about the wife who doesn't think she and her husband will ever be able to communicate any better than the daily, roommate-esque conversations? And what about the wife who feels like she has tried everything, but nothing seems to work? Is there hope? I say yes. A thousand times, yes!

If you're a wife who wants to improve her marriage by becoming a better communicator, let me assure you; you're in the right place. Primarily, I pray this book roots you first in the hope of Christ and his gospel, as he alone provides a strong enough foundation upon which to build. Secondly, and more practically, I pray this book equips you to think and act as a better communicator toward your husband based on biblical wisdom and its faithful application. In my view, this means becoming the type of wife that speaks carefully and with a mind to honor her husband as a means of obeying and glorifying Christ. If to you that sounds like a worthy goal,

I trust this book will deliver. But before you begin, a few things bear mentioning.

REASONS FOR THIS BOOK

The primary reason for writing this book is the conviction that God cares how wedded women communicate with their husbands. As believers in Christ, we should be quick to go to Scripture when dealing with all things marriage related—even and especially when it comes to how we communicate. We know in our heads that God cares how we speak, but many don't often take the two or three steps further to understand just how that applies at a heart-level within the marital covenant. The Bible has strong commands for how spouses should speak to each other, and the Holy Spirit is here to help us obey them. Why? Because God cares about how we speak—because how we speak indicates to a great extent what is taking place in our hearts. So, we take great care to speak and listen well because God desires it.

The next reason for this book is that it matters to couples. When we asked thousands of our readers and listeners what they struggled most with in marriage, the indisputable winner was communication. Not sex, not finances, not chores, and not even conflict. *Communication.* Why? Because every other area of dysfunction a couple faces always starts and persists through dysfunctional communication. If a couple can't meaningfully exchange soul-deep thoughts and feelings, how can they expect to solve soul-deep problems or feel soul-deep connection? Communication is the pipeline through which individuals connect, and many couples feel as if their pipes leak uncontrollably or are severed completely. Thus, this book. Communication is tough and it matters to real people like you and me.

That leads me to my third reason: By communication, marriages either flourish or die. If a couple can't communicate—by which I mean they can't share ideas, meaning, and experiences, not necessarily only through speech—then they can't meaningfully work through anything. Not sin, not frustration, not life's big questions, not even dinner plans. Without effective communication, marriages die on the vine. With it, they have a chance. This isn't to understate the necessity of gospel-centrality and Christ-like love—both are required—but only to say that communication quality is high on the list of determiners for marital success. It's a biblical notion borne out by research and data.[1]

THREE UNDERLYING PREMISES

Aside from assuming the truths of primary Christian doctrines (at a minimum this means affirming the Apostles' Creed), this book is written with three underlying premises.

Premise 1: A complementarian understanding of marriage

Stated briefly, I embrace the interpretation of Scripture—namely Genesis 1–3, Ephesians 5:22–33, and 1 Timothy 2:13—that regards the husband as the head of the home and the wife as his helper. This topic is still hotly debated, so I won't do so here aside from one clarifying statement: the biblical marital dynamic of head and helper is not one of power, position, or importance, but rather one concerning roles and responsibilities. When we hear words such as *submission* and *headship*, we might be tempted to read meaning into them that is more reflective of our culture than that of their original biblical audiences. Biblically, men and women

---

[1] https://www.researchgate.net/publication/324680369_Marital_Satisfaction_and_Communication_Skills_among_Married_Couples

are both made in the *imago Dei* and have equal value, worth, and importance. Head and helper distinctions are biblical ones, so we must seek to understand and apply them faithfully, regardless of how they go against the cultural grain.

This complementary relationship between husbands and wives led the apostles to write to married men and women of the early churches uniquely. For example, wives are given specific instruction regarding their adorning. Why didn't Peter write the below words to men and women alike? Consider his words to married women:

> "Don't let your beauty consist of outward things like elaborate hairstyles and wearing gold jewelry or fine clothes, but rather what is inside the heart— the imperishable quality of a gentle and quiet spirit, which is of great worth in God's sight. For in the past, the holy women who put their hope in God also adorned themselves in this way, submitting to their own husbands." (1 Peter 3:3–5 CSB)

He is speaking to the unique leanings within a woman's heart, just as in other places Peter and Paul speak to the inklings of men. For us, a gentle and quiet spirit will be reflected in our communication toward our husbands, but we must first submit ourselves to God and the authority of Scripture before we can hope to grow in this area. Gentle and quiet does not mean being weak-willed or functioning like a doormat. It means that a wife can be *uniquely* self-controlled and unwavering in how she communicates to her husband with both truth and love. Each chapter in this book seeks to help wives identify their unique tendencies and treat them biblically, but rest assured, Ryan's corresponding book for men will do the same for them.

Premise 2: Communication is a Grace of God

The ability to communicate—or, to share ideas, meaning, and experiences—with another soul is so common and familiar that we take it for granted. This is no doubt a major reason why we don't excel as well as we could. Communication is truly a gift and grace of God. You can use it as a tool to build up your husband, or you can misuse it for your own gain.

Consider the Tower of Babel. Their command of language enabled civilization to advance quickly, but instead of using their power to honor God, they decided to build a tower and make a name for themselves...*themselves!* (Genesis 11:4) Needless to say, it did not end well. "And the LORD said, 'Behold, they are one people, and they have all one language, and this is only the beginning of what they will do. And nothing that they propose to do will now be impossible for them. Come, let us go down and there confuse their language, so that they may not understand one another's speech" (Genesis 11:6–7). Chaos and confusion broke out—the building of the tower ceased, and people scattered.

Effective communication is powerful and it's a magnificent grace of God. May the Lord help us to communicate clearly and selflessly to our husbands and avoid unnecessary confusion or chaos in our marriage in the process. We will dive deeper into the grace and gift of communication in chapter one.

Premise 3: Communication is a Learnable Skill

Finally, communication skills are something you can learn. Whether consciously or not, many communicate however comes most quickly and naturally, failing to realize they can gain tangible skill in this area. You are not doomed to have the same marital communication culture your entire life! Both you and your husband can grow.

Of course, good communication is predicated on love, trust, and many other things, but how can we expect to build uncommon love and trust if we settle for common communication? Fierce wife, be encouraged! You *can* change, and you *can* grow into the kind of woman who communicates well, regardless of your past, personality, or predisposition. And, you *can* have a marriage that is marked by wonderful, functional, *uncommon* communication. More on this in chapter two.

BOOK STRUCTURE

Finally, knowing how the book is structured will help you get your bearings early and get the most from these pages.

Chapter Order

The order in which you read the chapters is flexible, as long as you read chapters one and two first. As mentioned above, those chapters establish our foundation, which will help the subsequent chapters make more sense. Feel free to read the other chapters in whatever order works best for you. I just ask that you read chapters one and two first.

Application Questions

Each chapter includes questions to help you think more deeply and personally about the material covered. At times this may include a challenge (ex. Writing a letter to your husband). I encourage you to view the questions as tools to be used at your discretion, so long as they prove beneficial. In other words, don't let the questions bog you down if you find yourself reading with limited time or energy. Get through the book however you choose, but do get through it.

Devotional Supplement?

There are eighteen chapters, which means this book could be used as a three-week study (assuming one day off per week). Each day includes Scripture to varying degrees, so you will see clear lines drawn from the topic into the pages of God's Word, but it is no replacement for your own daily scripture reading.

If you do decide to use this book as a three-week study, plan on ten to fifteen minutes of daily reading and another ten minutes for questions, in addition to your personal study and prayer times. I recommend setting aside Saturdays or Sundays as your off days.

AN ENCOURAGEMENT AS YOU GO

Nobody needs help communicating when things are going great. It's when things break down that couples realize they need help. And, many times, they don't fully realize exactly *what* they need. If communication is an ongoing problem, it's reasonable to not know how to put that exact problem into words. Which is precisely why you hold *these* words in your hand.

My entire goal for this book is to give you hope and tools for how you communicate and relate to your husband. Why? Because learning to communicate better with my husband changed our marriage in deep and lasting ways. I want to share that not just so you can be happier but so you can live more united and on mission with Christ. Our King is worthy, and his eternal work awaits.

Sadly, we've seen too many men and women sidelined by marital misfires. A miscommunication unaddressed turns to frustration, frustration to bitterness, bitterness to isolation, and isolation to prolonged marital strife or an affair. It's tragic, but common. My hope is that by learning skills to prevail against dysfunction, distraction, and diversions, you will be able to get *at* your husband's heart. To know him, to love him, and to submit to him in such a way that he *feels* known, loved, and respected.

With all of that, I'd be honored to pray for you.

> *Father, you alone are God, and you alone are worthy of all glory. Thank you for the magnificent gift of knowing you and being known by you. And thank you for the Word you've revealed that we might know your will.*
>
> *Please, be with this woman as she learns more about how to love her husband through communication. Open her eyes, soften her heart, and teach her to value what you value: gentleness, love, and submission. Make her attentive to your word and diligent to apply all it instructs. I pray the coming weeks and months would be formative for her—so much so that her husband not only sees her change but feels it as well. Guide her, bless her, sustain her, and more than anything, be with her. We pray your will be done, Father, on earth as it is in heaven.*
>
> *All this I pray in the glorious name of Jesus Christ. Amen.*
>
> *Selena*

CHAPTER ONE

Your Communication Garden

The Lord is my shepherd; I shall not want.
He makes me lie down in green pastures.
He leads me beside still waters. He restores my soul.
He leads me in paths of righteousness
for his name's sake.
Psalm 23:1–3

In its most essential form, communication means sharing information and ideas with another. It is both a common grace and a powerful tool from God; one we must be careful not to mishandle in marriage.

By common grace, I mean that everyone in the world has been given the ability to communicate. A new baby cries to communicate a need; a toddler squeals with joy to communicate her excitement on the playground, and a wife smiles sweetly to her husband, telling him how much she adores him while they head out for a date. Everyone *can* communicate, and it is a powerful tool we can wield for either the good or harm of those around us.

What we say, when we say it, and how we say it (or don't say it) will communicate *something* and the challenges come when we don't communicate how the Bible instructs. Instead, we give way to our emotions and let them take the helm—steering our relational ship straight into the rocky shore. Another way we sabotage our communication in marriage is that we assume we don't need help, like somehow, we will figure it out eventually, and there's no need to put any real effort into it. Most likely, that's not you if you're reading this book.

Either way, we need to learn to wield the tool of communication with wisdom, charity, and love. We must learn to value the art of communication and understand the power it has in unifying or dividing us from our spouse. Learning how to communicate in a way that reaches the heart of your husband is not easy, but it is worth it. I compare it to planting a garden in the early spring. You begin with seeds or starts, and while you don't see the fruit of the seeds yet, the potential is there! The tomato seed you planted will grow tomatoes, even if you don't see them right away. A garden needs water, time, sunshine, and care—careful pruning, weed pulling, and pest killing.

Though you're likely aware that your marital communication garden needs to be watered and fed, it's not a skill that comes as naturally as many assume. It's a skill that requires time to be practiced and learned, and probably more than you think. In many ways failure is imminent, but the wise persevere, trusting the fruit will come. Give it time. And tend to the weeds—those familiar responses that choke out the life of your communication—because weeds destroy fruit. Most important, go to the Son—the Word who was with God in the beginning. He is your faithful and patient Shepherd, calling you on in your journey.

I pray this book would support and affirm everything the Lord is already teaching you through your personal Bible study. May you be encouraged and challenged by each chapter, and may you be equipped for how to apply biblical wisdom to your communication "garden."

Remember, he has given you everything you need for this journey. He will sustain, lead, and restore you—for His glory and your good.

REFLECT

Take a moment to reflect on past conversations that led to conflict with your husband. Now filter through those conflicts to see which ones began because you said something one of you thought was benign but the other took it the wrong way. He heard your quickness as harshness and responded in a way that you didn't expect (or vice versa)—why? Why did he take issue with something you said when you didn't mean to offend him? If couples literally injured one another as often as they do figuratively with their words, they'd both have season passes to the nearest dock-in-a-box!

Even after more than twenty years together, Ryan and I continue to experience these types of conflicts in our communication. We forget about things like tone, motivation, definition of words versus how we use it (meaning versus intent), timing, and location. All these matter. If we don't take care to understand some of these foundational pieces, then we will continue to wearily fight the same battles while simultaneously chipping away at our unity and joy.

Forging ahead and foolishly forgetting our Shepherd's words about love, patience, and kindness allows weeds to take root and threaten the communication fruit we worked so diligently to cultivate.

WORDS MATTER

Ryan likes to remind me that "words matter!" He especially likes to do this when we are in a rare but heated moment of conflict. Typically after I have said something hurtful or disrespectful, he will pick out a word or phrase that I said and define it for me. He will then ask me if this was how I intended to use the word. If it was, then he would explain to me how hurtful I was being (from his perspective). But if I didn't intend for that word or phrase to be used in that way, then he would tell me how I need to use the words I *meant* because *words matter.*

He is a better arguer than me and this is one of his tactics. God is growing and sanctifying us both and the reason I share is not to blame my husband or highlight his faults. Rather, I want to point out how he is right on at least one level: words *do* matter; definitions *do* matter. The heart's motivation behind the words also matters. Each piece matters, especially when it comes to communication in marriage.

If we speak flippantly or carelessly to our husbands, we are in danger of treating them in a way that dishonors God and dishonors them. How you speak, what you say, your posture, motivation, tone— how you listen and when you respond—it *all* matters.

KNOW YOUR SHEPHERD

Your ability to communicate well with your husband *must* be rooted first and foremost in your understanding of the gospel. Do you know who God is? Do you know who you are because of who God is? Granted, these are deep theological truths to explore, but they are also foundational to the Christian life.

If you don't first understand who God is, then you will have trouble knowing who you are and why you were created. Lack of understanding will result in wishy washy, feelings-based communication with your husband when it doesn't have to.

The New City Catechism (shorter version) teaches that God is the Creator of everyone and everything. Do you know and believe this in your gut? Being King and Creator of everything would then put me in one of two categories: submissive, adopted child—or rebellious unbeliever. Both will bear fruit. The question is, what type of fruit?

Submitting and entrusting our days to Jesus, our Shepherd, is not easy, but it is worth it. Remembering that it is he who pulled me out of sin, who called me out of death and into light—I can't help but respond with gratefulness and joyful obedience.

On the days when my joy *feels* lacking, and obedience *feels* hard, I can submit and surrender those feelings to God. I can then walk obediently, knowing that the Holy Spirit is producing his fruit in me: love, joy, patience, peace, kindness, goodness, faithfulness, gentleness, and self-control.

Knowledge of God is the ground from which healthy communication takes seed, grows, and blooms.

HOW CAN I KNOW GOD?

By his grace he has given us his twofold word: his Son (the incarnate word) and the written word (Scripture). God also reveals something about himself through the majesty of Creation. To quote

Ryan's communication book for husbands (because he writes it so perfectly and yes, I'm completely biased),

> "God made everything in such a way that it all resonates unceasingly with his splendor. His divine craftsmanship is so obviously visible in creation, that to summarize Job, "beasts and bushes teach of God's goodness and birds and fish declare it!" He is so abundantly evident that Job finally erupts, "Who among all these does not know that the hadn't of the LORD has done this?" Without uttering a word or sharing a thought, creation bellows without pause the magnificence of God, and this majestic music is readily heard by those with ears to hear it."[2]

Amen, and amen!

WORDS FORM COVENANTS

In the Old Testament, God makes covenants with his people through words. Presuming you are a wife reading this book, then the same is true for you: your marriage covenant with your husband began on your wedding day when you said your vows to your husband and sealed your marriage covenant before God and man. Your vows communicated your commitment to your lifelong marriage covenant. Again, our words carry weight and can either be wielded as a weapon or a tool.

---

2. Ryan Frederick, *How a Husband Speaks* (Tacoma, WA: Lion Press, 2023), 9.

BEAUTIFUL SUBMISSION

Below we will read the familiar marriage passage from Ephesians 5 about submission. As you read this passage, remember that we are wives who seek clarity and instruction from God on how to cultivate our communication garden with our husband. Meaning and purpose are found in words like *respect* and *submission*.

Ephesians 5:22, "Wives, submit to your own husbands, as to the Lord." Christ calls wives to submit to their own husbands as the Head, just as he/Christ is the head of the church. Submission in how a wife communicates to her husband is powerful and beautiful. It is powerful in that she can either affirm him as the head of their home and of their marriage covenant, or she can emasculate him by letting her emotions control her flesh-filled responses. Remember, Ephesians 5 is a call to both husbands and wives to submit and die to their "self" or flesh.

Submitting to a godly, loving husband who dies to himself and gives himself up for you regularly should not be difficult. Submitting to a husband who is not submitting himself to Christ (whether he is tyrannical, passive, or self-absorbed) is difficult, but not impossible. God can still use you and your biblical submission to him as a witness (1 Peter 3:1) while you find sufficiency in Christ.

Read further a few more verses (Ephesians 5:33) where Paul ends the chapter addressing both the husband and the wife:

"However, let each one of you love his wife as himself, and let the wife see that she respects her husband." The call for the wife is clear: love your husband by showing him respect. How? In your behavior, actions and most especially, in your words and how you communicate to him.

Submission is a beautiful picture of marriage when both the husband and the wife have submitted their lives first to God, and then to loving each other selflessly. Granted, we won't do this perfectly because we are still sinners undergoing the lifelong process of sanctification, but we must fight to live, love, and speak as Christ did all three. This, so that we might glorify our Lord, enjoy marriage, and be a light to unbelievers (John 13:35).

More on submission and communication later in the book.

WOULD YOU DIE FOR HIM?

One of our family's favorite verses is Acts 20:24, "But I do not account my life of any value nor as precious to myself, if only I may finish my course and ministry that I received from the Lord Jesus, to testify to the gospel of the grace of God." Paul is not talking specifically about marriage, but the meaning is the same for the Believer: death to the flesh is unto the glory of Christ!

But what of the wife who has an unsaved husband or one who fails to love her as Christ instructed? Peter has an apt encouragement, "Likewise, wives, be subject to your own husbands, so that *even if some do not obey the word*, they may be won without a word by the conduct of their wives, when they see your respectful and pure conduct" (1 Peter 3:1–2, emphasis added).

Respect and pure conduct are your tools to win your husband over to Christ. No wife can save her husband's soul; God alone is the one who can do that. But He can use your efforts of respecting him through your words and behavior to call your husband to him. Trust your Shepherd; you lack nothing you need for life and godliness (2 Peter 1:3) and he is faithful to lead, guide, sustain, and care for you.

Christ modeled ultimate sacrificial love by dying for us while we were still sinners. I pray that by his grace we too can learn to love our husbands sacrificially and submissively through how we communicate to them.

YOUR WORDS ARE POWERFUL

Fierce wife, your words carry immense power in the heart of your husband. Remember, your words can:
- Build him up or tear him down.
- Equip him to lead or cause him to quit trying.
- Encourage and embolden his faith or cut him down producing fear and insecurity.
- Be filled with grace, or weighty with contempt and disdain.
- God cares how you communicate to your husband. What you say and how you say it matters.

My prayer is that you and your husband will experience oneness that is deep, rich, and lasting. When you choose to respond and communicate in gentleness, kindness, love, patience, respect, and joyful submission—you choose to not only honor him, but to honor and glorify your heavenly Father. Your garden will flourish with fruit for generations when you know and trust your Shepherd.

> **KEY TAKEAWAY**
>
> Communication is a grace of God, and godly communication requires wisdom, charity, and love as modeled by Christ and enabled by the Holy Spirit.

MEDIOCRITY VS. MASTERY

Mediocrity	*Mastery*
Communciates based on emotions or feelings	Acknowledges feelings and emotions, but chooses to speak with wisdom
Cringes at the idea of submitting to the Lord in how she speaks to her husband	Embraces submitting to the Lord in her speech to her husband
"I'll respect my husband when he deserves it!"	Trusts and obeys God in how she respects her husband

APPLICATION QUESTIONS

What is one way I can stop letting my feelings and emotions take charge of how I communicate with my husband?

How can I submit and help my husband in how I speak to him?

When has God sustained and anchored me during past conflicts with my husband?

CHAPTER TWO

The Words of an Excellent Wife

An excellent wife who can find?
She is far more precious than jewels.
The heart of her husband trusts in her,
and he will have no lack of gain.
Proverbs 31:10–11

Communication is a skill that can be learned and even mastered, but if it is done without love it's in vain. It won't matter how skilled you are; your husband's ears might hear you, but his heart won't trust you.

PROVERBS 31 AND THE GOSPEL

Praise God for not leaving us to our own vices. He is good and gracious to instruct, equip and empower us to be skilled communicators who love their husbands in such a way that he trusts her completely. Thus, she is worth *far* more than precious jewels.

Why is a godly wife described in Proverbs 31 as being worth more than precious jewels? It's interesting to read this section of

Scripture because you get the sense that the author is praising and speaking of a woman he's known for a lifetime. The language is one of familiarity.

One of the challenges of Proverbs 31 (beyond its familiarity) is that it can feel crushing. Who even is this woman? She's superhuman. If we read it as a list of "shoulds," it either puffs us up in sinful and unsustainable self-righteousness or it crushes us with unattainable perfection. So, how shall we read it? Not as a list of prescriptions for would-be godly women, but as a description of a woman whose identity is secure in her heavenly Father. Consider how that woman is described: (Read Proverbs 31:10–31).

- Her husband trust her with his heart (31:11)
- "She does him good, and not harm, all the days of her life" (31:12)
- She works willingly, diligently, and is not afraid of a big task (31:13)
- She prepares and provides for her family and home: early in the morning and late into the evening (31:15)
- She makes herself strong (31:17)
- She understands worth (31:18)
- She opens her hand; reaching for the needy and giving to the poor (31:20)
- She is not afraid of the future, or the seasons, but laughs at the time to come (31:21)
- She is not idle (31:19, 22)
- "She opens her mouth with wisdom, and the teaching of kindness is on her tongue." (31:26)
- Her children value her, calling her "blessed" (31:28)
- Her husband praises her (31:29)

- ♦ She fears the Lord (31:30)

Sounds idyllic and unattainable, and without God, none of us stand a chance at ever *being* a woman who might be described like this. Instead, the Proverbs 31 woman should be a spotlight, drawing our attention to the fact that this is the *description* of a *woman who fears the Lord*. She and her superhuman abilities are not the goal...*he* is.

THE TWENTY-FIRST CENTURY, GOD-FEARING WOMAN

What might this God-fearing woman look like in our modern reality? Imagine this scenario: she's picking up her kids from school, everyone is tired and a bit cranky. She's not having their attitudes, so she snaps at them to set them straight. She forgot to plan dinner and isn't sure what to cook, and oops! She forgot they were having friends over for dinner tonight. After she gets home and scrambles to find something from the freezer, hubby walks in, asking about her day as he trips over the mountain of laundry and reaches for his crying baby (this may or may not be an example from my own life that seemed suitable here). How does a Proverbs 31 woman respond in this scenario? How would you respond? Most importantly, from which well might she drink in this moment of drought?

I imagine that a God-fearing woman might stress a little in this case (ok, I'm projecting because I would), but ideally, she wouldn't let it ruin how she responds to her husband.

Let's rewind this scene and see how it could play out differently. Instead of snapping at her children's attitudes, she calmly hugs each of them, reassuring them that she sees them and loves them. As for Laundry Mountain, well, she just must laugh rather than stew about it. As she stashes it out of sight, she smiles and sighs. She knows that lots of laundry means there is a lot of life in her home!

Can we ever be that Proverbs 31 woman who fears the Lord if we're struggling through the day rather than conquering it? One thousand percent, yes. How? Because we don't have to rely on our own strength. Paul reminds us that it's in our weakness that Christ's power is made perfect in us. (2 Corinthians 12:9–10) Responding from a place of trust is vastly different from responding out of lack and insecurity.

There is joy to be found in the work and he will strengthen you for it. By living securely in his love, you are freed up to stumble through your days, with joy for your children and love for your husband.

Security in Christ helps us speak and act in ways that reflect the Father's love. Therefore, we can trust the Holy Spirit to produce fruit during our seasons of chaos. The Proverbs 31 woman's attributes come from the deep well of the Father's love and saving grace—they well up from within rather than being mustered from without.

There is something in her air and manner that reflects the love of the Father and the transforming work of the Holy Spirit. He changes everything about her very *being*, and that transforms everything about her *doing*, especially in how she communicates her love and respect for her husband.

This is how you begin to move the needle when it comes to communication in your marriage. When God is at work in your life, the old, self-reliant, lazy ways of communication will fall away. In 2 Corinthians 5:17–19, the apostle Paul provides us with a vivid reminder of the new creation we are in Christ and what that means,

> "Therefore, if anyone is in Christ, he is a new creation. The old has passed away; behold, the new has come. All this is from God, who through Christ reconciled us to himself and gave us the

ministry of reconciliation; that is, in Christ God was reconciling the world to himself, not counting their trespasses against them, and entrusting to us the message of reconciliation."

As new creations in Christ, our sins and old ways have passed away, which means it is time for us to begin living like it. When we fail, run to God and repent and then run to your husband and repent. Seek reconciliation and restoration quickly.

When we live out of our newly created lives, we learn how to recognize "old ways" such as poor communication in our marriage. As God continues his sanctifying work in us, he is faithful to instruct us on how to wield our words wisely—as tools rather than weapons.

FOR THE REST OF YOUR COMMUNICATION JOURNEY

As with all things Fierce Marriage or Ryan-and-Selena related, we pray that in sharing our own communication struggles, we will decrease and Christ will increase.

Here are a few reminders for you as you embark on your journey through the rest of this book.

1. 1 Corinthians 13:1 "If I speak in tongues of men and of angels, but have not love, I am a noisy gong or a clanging cymbal." Communication is a skill you can learn, but godly communication requires love.
2. The gospel changes everything. Know him and run *first* to him—he is the Living Water that sustains you.
3. Take time, through prayer and reading the Scriptures, to reflect on sin/struggles in your communication with your

husband. Repent as needed and reflect on what God desires to do in your marriage through your communication.
4. Remember your words are not weapons, but tools to be wielded skillfully by a woman who fears the Lord.
5. Be brave, fierce wife! God has already equipped and readied you for this journey. Learn to communicate to your husband as the Father communicates with you: in love.

Put on love, which binds everything together in perfect harmony. And let the peace of Christ rule in your hearts, to which indeed you were called in one body. And be thankful.
Colossians 3:15

> **KEY TAKEAWAY**
>
> Communication is a skill that can be learned for the glory of God and the good of your marriage. The Proverbs 31 woman is a wife who knows and fears the Lord, her identity is anchored in him, and is empowered to skillfully communicate despite the craziness of life.

MEDIOCRITY VS. MASTERY

Mediocrity	*Mastery*
Self-reliant	Christ-reliant
Responds to stress by being hasty and harsh in her communication;	Responds from a place of being rooted in Christ
Comfortable retaining old communication habits	Humbly embraces "new" ways of speaking to her husband

APPLICATION QUESTIONS

Do you consider yourself to be a "Proverbs 31" wife? Why or why not? Reflect on the difference between interpreting the chapter as "prescriptive" vs. "descriptive."

Does your husband trust you with his heart in how he communicates to you? Why or why not, and how can you tell?

When your days are crazy, do you respond to your husband out of your own strength, or do you rely on God's strength? How can you tell?

CHAPTER THREE

Off with the Old; On with the New

*Put on then, as God's chosen ones, holy and
beloved, compassionate hearts, kindness, humility,
meekness, and patience, bearing with one another and, if
one has a complaint against another, forgiving each
other; as the Lord has forgiven you, so you also must
forgive. And above all these put on love, which binds
everything together in perfect harmony. And let the peace
of Christ rule in your hearts, to which indeed you were
called in one body. And be thankful.*
Colossians 3:12–15

The greatest instigator of poor communication is not our minds or emotions; it's our flesh. This is why in a previous chapter I discussed how the gospel changes how we use words because the love of God transforms our hearts, calling us out of selfishness and fear into selflessness and freedom.

Conceptually, this makes sense. As we walk with Jesus more closely, we resemble him more clearly. However, what exactly does it look like to walk in freedom and confidence in how you communicate with your husband? That's a fundamental question to answer if we are to love our husbands not only "in word or talk but in deed and in truth" (1 John 3:18).

Practicing the love of God in marital communication requires a functional, radical shift in your heart's lordship. Is Christ the Lord of your tongue, or is it yourself? As we will explore, Christ's lordship means we must submit even our emotions to him as we die to our flesh through responding in a Spirit-led manner instead of a self-infused one. Paul calls this putting *off* the old and putting *on* the new, so let's take a closer look at what he means.

GETTING ON WITH PUTTING OFF

After urging the church at Colossae to fight against "indulgence of the flesh" (Colossians 2:23), Paul reminds them how to tangibly live out that calling in everyday life. Consider the passage below:

> *If then you have been raised with Christ, seek the things that are above, where Christ is, seated at the right hand of God. Set your minds on things that are above, not on things that are on earth. For you have died, and your life is hidden with Christ in God. When Christ who is your life appears, then you also will appear with him in glory. Put to death therefore what is earthly in you: sexual immorality, impurity, passion, evil desire, and covetousness, which is idolatry. On account of these the wrath of God is coming. In these you too once walked, when you were living in them. But now you must put them all away: anger, wrath, malice, slander, and obscene talk from*

your mouth. Do not lie to one another, seeing that you have put off the old self with its practices...

(Colossians 3:1–9, emphasis added)

Cold legalism and moralism are not enough to change behavior; they don't change the heart, only Christ does that. Thus, the Colossians needed the reminder, and so do we! The order of Paul's encouragement is helpful to note as we unpack this passage further.

The first thing Paul does is lift their eyes and remind them of their identity through the *if* statement. "If, then you have been raised in Christ" (Colossians 3:1). He's setting up the rest of the chapter with the single grounding reality applicable only to believers in Jesus. For those who are *in Christ*—which I will assume as Paul does, that my reader is—the rest follows. The reason I bring attention to it here is that if we try to do what follows without being united with Christ, it won't work. At least not in a lasting way. So, fierce wife, we start there. Are you, in fact, "raised with Christ"? If you are, this is your call to remember that grounding reality as we continue down the passage.

Second, Paul continues with the *then* part of the clause. Therefore "seek the things that are above, where Christ is" (Colossians 3:2). Here is a charge to the Colossians to lift their focus consciously, intentionally toward heavenly, eternal reality of our reigning Christ rather than being consumed by things below, such as irritations, frustrations, justified anger, and whatever else would steal your gaze. Instead of accepting the junk that sits right in front of us, we are taught to seek gold above. We seek and we set our minds on it. It's a deliberate determination; dogged, even. I don't know about you, but I need this reminder *especially* in the exact moments

I'm tempted to communicate unlovingly (in my flesh) toward my husband. Let's keep going.

Thirdly, Paul gives the *why*. He says, "*for* you have died, and your life is hidden with Christ in God." Christ has laid claim to your very life, and only he can because he has already given his. But just as he gave his life, he conquered death, and his promise to those who are in him is that they will be raised with him again in glory. That, friend, is your reason *why* as well as your functional *how*. Because you are in Christ, you can fix your eyes on Christ, because you belong to Christ, even unto glory. If there's a more worthy reason to lay my communication sins and idols at his feet, I haven't found it.

Finally, we get to the putting off part. The main thrust of Paul's "put off" encouragement culminates here. He writes, "Put to death therefore what is earthly in you." If we are truly raised with Christ and called blameless in him, that spiritual reality should have non-spiritual evidence. This doesn't mean we're sinless, but it certainly means we sin less. (See what I did there?) Perfection won't happen until Christ's return, but his imminence should have present perfecting effects. In other words, as God's chosen ones, "holy and beloved" (vs. 12), we are certain to have distinctive ways of living that set us apart as his people.

One of those ways of living involves the things we put to death, "sexual immorality, impurity, *passion*, evil desire, and covetousness, which is idolatry…*anger, wrath, malice, slander*, and *obscene talk from your mouth. Do not lie* to one another, seeing that you have put off the old self with its practices" (Colossians 3:5–9, emphasis added). Did you catch those italicized words? Passion, anger, wrath, malice, slander, obscenity, and lies. It seems that there is much putting-to-death when it comes to areas of emotion and communication!

Are you putting to death your earthly responses when tensions are high and your flesh wars against the Spirit? Do you love and communicate with your husband in a way that reflects that which is earthly in you? Or does it reflect the Holy Spirit within you? Do you *act* as one who has been raised with Christ, a child of God, holy and beloved?

THE WAGES OF LIFE

Without Christ, we are dead in our sin. But in Christ, death is not your inheritance, but life. The trick is living like it! Paul wrote to the Romans, "How can we who died to sin still live in it? Do you not know that all of us who have been baptized into Christ Jesus were baptized into his death? We were buried therefore with him by baptism into death, in order that, just as Christ was raised from the dead by the glory of the Father, *we too might walk in newness of life*" (Romans 6:2–4, emphasis added).

So, though the wages of sin is death, the wages of life in Christ is salvation, which should mean the steady death of sin in us (Romans 3:23; 6:2). And this is not by our own strength, but by the power of the promised Spirit who Christ sent to help us to this worthy end. So, may your speech to your husband no longer be characterized by what is dead in you, but by the abundant life that is rightfully yours in Christ.

But *abundant life* is such a general idea. What does that specifically mean in the life of a Christian wife? We've put off sin; now what shall we put on? Paul addresses just that a few verses down.

> *Put on then, as God's chosen ones, holy and beloved, compassionate hearts, kindness, humility, meekness, and patience, bearing with one another and, if one has a complaint against another, forgiving each other; as the Lord has forgiven you, so you also must forgive. And above all these put on love, which binds everything together in perfect harmony. And let the peace of Christ rule in your hearts, to which indeed you were called in one body. And be thankful.* (Colossians 3:12–15)

A wife who is dependent on and secure in the Lord is eager—quick, even—to learn to let the peace of Christ rule, even and especially when she is angry, frustrated, tired, or hurt. It's his loving rulership that adorns and equips her to love her husband in an otherworldly way. That is how we put on godly attributes, by remembering Whose we are.

Remember, it's not always an automatic flip of the switch. It takes time to learn to put on the things of God, but He is patient and has placed you in your marriage covenant to grow and be sanctified. So, though you will fail, you fail forward and into the arms of your forgiving Lord. But the often unmentioned key to failing forward is fast repentance. It's not easy, and it will feel wrong to your flesh, but it's Christ's way forward, which means it's the best way.

HIS PROMISE AWAITS

Friend, if you're in Christ, God has saved you. Therefore, sin has been put to death in you. But you must put off the old and put on the new. With each opportunity God gives you and your spouse, you have the chance to do just that. Learn to trust God and submit your earthly responses to Him. "Therefore do not throw away your confidence, which has a great reward. For you have need of endurance, so that when you have done the will of God you may receive what is promised" (Hebrews 10:35–36). So, fellow wife, do not throw away your confidence, put off your old self, and respond how he has responded to you: in love. His promise awaits, even in your communication life with your husband.

> **KEY TAKEAWAY**
>
> In many ways, the process of growing into a better communicator is one of putting off your old self and putting on the new.

MEDIOCRITY VS. MASTERY

Mediocrity	*Mastery*
Seeks her own gain	Seeks eternal gain rather than temporary gratification
Unable or unwilling to cast off her old self	Unafraid to put on her "new" self who is in Christ
Trusts her ability to fix or figure out communication problems	Trusts that God is transforming her words through her relationship with him

APPLICATION QUESTIONS

Do the words you speak to your husband reflect your new life in Christ? Why or why not?

Write down two or three "old" ways you have communicated to your husband.

Write down two or three "new" ways that will replace (or put to death) the "old" ways of communicating.

CHAPTER FOUR

Destroying Manipulation in Your Marriage

For there is no distinction: for all have sinned and fall short of the glory of God, and are justified by his grace as a gift, through the redemption that is in Christ Jesus.
Romans 3:22–24

In our years helping couples, Ryan and I have found reason to spend many hours studying manipulation tactics and their effects on marriage. Early on, what we found was as weighty as it was eye opening, and not just because manipulation tactics are so pervasive, but because they were being used by us, in our own marriage!

It isn't that we were knowingly using underhanded means to control each other, but that we had settled into patterns of relating to one another that didn't pass the manipulation sniff-test. He discovered his own manipulative tendencies, and I was able to identify some of mine, so we began the process of uprooting our manipulative tendencies. Our efforts produced great fruit, but it took thick skin, persistence, and lots of honesty.

Why? Because manipulation is a sneaky, covert sin. And when it's present in marriage, it lurks quietly in the darkness, hidden by the passage of time and spousal familiarity. Victims of manipulation tactics struggle to see them at work, and speaking from experience, manipulators themselves can also be clueless of how they've learned to creatively craft the narrative to serve them best.

In our time serving couples, we've addressed most issues relevant to Christian marriage, but nothing has surprised us quite like the revelation that *everyone* is capable of manipulation. Every husband and every wife can become a manipulator. How? Because manipulation is so subtle. It's all too easy for it to creep into even the healthiest marriages.

For clarity, psychologists define manipulation as a form of emotional abuse aimed at controlling the other person. There are numerous common manipulation tactics used in relationships, and I'll walk through many of them below. First, I need to ask: Are you a manipulator in your marriage? Like me, your first reaction may be a resounding *no*. It's natural to think, *there's no way I'm the manipulator*. Based on the above definition, who wants to be called controlling and abusive? Not me! Still, even this area of your heart must not be immune to careful introspection.

THE BAD NEWS IS BAD, BUT THE GOOD NEWS IS BETTER

For starters, consider the passage included at the start of this chapter: "all have sinned and fall short of the glory of God" (Romans 3:23). *All* includes you and me while *sin* is aptly described as outright rebellion against God. Isaiah said that even the good things we do are like "filthy rags" (Isaiah 64:6) when compared to the holiness of God. This means that even the most well-intentioned wife is capable of emotionally manipulating and seeking to control her husband or usurp his headship in the home. Even a well-intentioned, Bible-reading, God-fearing woman is capable of being a manipulator without knowing it. This was the exact revelation that floored me. But the story doesn't end there, thank God.

Confronting your ability to sin in worse ways than you realize will either crush you or cast you headlong into the grace of God. You'll die under its load or retreat into the arms of your heavenly Father. Thank God the passage doesn't end with "all have sinned and fall short." Instead, Paul goes on, saying that those same sinners "are justified by his grace *as a gift*, through the redemption that is in Christ Jesus" (Romans 3:23, emphasis added). Yes, the bad news is bad, but I'm happy to say the good news is better!

The bad news is that you're capable of grievous sin (v. 23), but the Good News is that Christ has saved you from the bondage of sin and is calling you to walk in his righteousness (v. 24). This goes for both you and your husband, and you both need the same grace available in Christ! My prayer is that by learning about your own potential to form manipulation habits, you can root them out and walk in new levels of truth and love. Let's look at seven common manipulation habits next.

SEVEN COMMON MANIPULATION TACTICS

In our research and experience, seven commonly used manipulation tactics have bubbled to the surface. As you read through each tactic, I encourage you to take an honest assessment of your communication habits with your husband. Try to focus on yourself, *not* your husband, as you read them. (Don't worry; if he's reading *How a Husband Speaks*, he'll be asking the same questions of himself.) Fair warning, some of the below might sound a bit technical. This is because precise language is needed to really pin down these slippery tactics.

Do any of the below sound familiar?

1) Triangulation

This kind of manipulation happens when, to help make their case, one spouse cites friends, coworkers, or other biased references to add credibility and social pressure favoring their side of an issue. Examples include saying something like, "Everyone thinks that…" or, as a wife might say, "Cathy's husband lets her go out with the girls; why won't you?" Or, she could argue, "Paul took his family to Maui last year, so why can't we go?"

The triangulator's objective is clear to them, and they'll build a case by including agreeing opinions from friends and others to make the other feel like they're on the wrong side of the issue. Not only that, but they'll also exclude dissenting opinions intentionally because they'd only weaken their case.

Have you ever triangulated to win an argument?

2) Moving the Goalposts

This tactic includes changing the rules of conversation by demanding greater or different evidence for the other person to refute your claim. It's like changing the subject because it displaces the basis of the conversation and confuses the efforts of the other.

This tactic also includes blaming your spouse for something or making demands to alleviate your frustration, then upping the demands once they've been met.

Imagine a wife who spends most of her time on her phone (social media, online shopping, pick your poison) and away from the family. Frustrated, her husband voices his concerns, to which she responds, "You never seem like you want to talk," or "You're on your phone all the time." After weeks of his attempts at starting conversations, she still spends just as much time disengaged and on her phone. When he confronts her again, she either says he didn't try hard enough, she didn't know, or she creates some other reason or way for him to fix it. The goal posts have moved, and the husband feels more disconnected than ever.

Have you ever moved the goalposts?

3) *Gaslighting*

Gaslighters invalidate individuals and arguments by making the other person question their memory, identity, or even reality itself. By persistently questioning and rewriting history, the gaslighter gains power in the relationship because the other person's confidence has been undermined so thoroughly that they no longer trust their own intuitions or judgements.

Key gaslighting phrases include, "You're overreacting," "You're imagining things," "I never said," "It's not a big deal," or "I only did that because I love you." Gaslighters will often have very selective memories and will weaponize trust and privacy to isolate others from objective community. "How could you tell him that? You've violated my privacy." Sure, some boundaries are healthy, but gaslighters will often use boundaries to keep toxic things in, when healthy boundaries are all about keeping toxicity out.

Gaslighting comes in both subtle and overt forms and those who do it may or may not be aware that they're doing it. This form of manipulation is especially harmful in marriage because it erodes trust and confidence while enthroning one spouse as the arbiter of reality in the relationship. Gaslighters are frequently narcissists.

Are you a gaslighter?

4) *Dismissiveness*

A dismissive spouse will seek to undercut the other person's assertions or accomplishments by invalidating them or through disingenuous argumentation. The main issue with dismissiveness is that it doesn't allow the main source of contention enough time or space to be worked through fully.

Examples include telling your husband he's just upset because he's hungry or tired instead of owning the fact that something you did warrants his frustration (and an apology from you). Another example would be nitpicking an argument and invalidating it because a word was used imprecisely or incorrectly.

Are you dismissive toward your husband?

5) *Projection*

Projection is when one person attributes their own feelings or desires to the other person as a means of masking or distracting from their own similar feelings.

Examples include one spouse blaming the other for being too worried about money when they're the one who is typically first to fear lack, or the habitually critical wife who claims that everything her husband says is some form of critique. Another example is a wife who obsesses about her husband's faithfulness—which can materialize as jealousy or distrust—while she secretly and frequently flirts with men online or at work.

Projecting one's own negative traits onto the other is a psychological defense mechanism where the person doing the projecting seeks to shift focus and therefore, blame, to the other person as a means of making themselves feel better.

Do you project your own negative traits onto your husband?

6) Treating Like a Child

This is a subcategory of gaslighting that specifically makes the other person doubt their ability to handle responsibility or question their own intellect. By treating the other person like a child—often using patronizing, sarcastic, or condescending language—the manipulator convinces their spouse to "let them handle" whatever situation is in question.

Examples include constantly nagging your husband even though he assures you he heard you and will take care of whatever it is you're nagging him about. Another example is a wife who never leaves her husband in charge of anything, not even the kids, because she can't bear the thought of him fathering in a way that is different from her mothering. Part of this might be that your husband objectively lacks maturity, but it could also be a bid for control.

In general, this is a form of talking down to the other person that causes them to doubt their abilities and instead default to dependance or codependence on the manipulator. This makes the manipulator feel useful, valued, and most importantly, in control.

Do you treat your husband like a child?

7) The Silent Treatment

The name says it all. While some time of quietness after an argument is healthy and natural to help a husband or wife process their thoughts and feelings, giving someone the silent treatment is a weaponized version of this.

A spouse who uses the silent treatment cuts off communication to punish their spouse during or after a conflict. The connection-starved spouse eventually "breaks" by conceding their side of the argument to reinstate the relationship and experience peace once again.

Do you give your husband the silent treatment?

THE FOUR RS

I don't know about you, but I was personally shocked and convicted by the number of subtle and not-so-subtle manipulation habits I had deployed over the years. Do any of the above sound familiar to you? And, as a wife, what should you do about them? Here are four tangible steps to root out manipulation in your communication. The following Application Questions will guide you further.

1. Recognize

You can't begin to make progress until you have an accurate diagnosis. My hope is that this chapter helped you understand how a few manipulation tactics could function in a marriage. But recognition can't start and end with yourself. Blind spots are far too difficult to self-diagnose. You need God, your husband, and godly women to help. Do some reflecting, then ask those you trust to help you see yourself and your behavior objectively. Try to accurately give an account of a past argument or situation that smells like manipulation. Then, ask them what they think. The next part is the tricky part: it's not enough for them to see it, you must see it too, and own it. Doing so will lead naturally to the next step.

2. Repent

Once you recognize and take responsibility for your tendencies and faults in this area, confess them to God, ask for forgiveness, and turn toward righteousness. He stands ready to forgive, love, and teach you to walk in lockstep with the Holy Spirit. Repent and repent quickly. Then, after repenting to God, it's time to begin mending earthly relationships.

3. Reconcile

The first time Ryan called me out on a manipulation tactic I was (unknowingly) using, I denied it. After our argument, I talked to Ryan and admitted how *maybe* I had used manipulation tactics in our marriage, and I just had not been made aware of it. The whole conversation was disarming. He felt seen and expressed his gratitude. I asked him for forgiveness, then I asked for his help. He graciously agreed, and we've since created a culture where we're both able to recognize and confess manipulation tactics that would have previously been left to fester, which is the next step.

4. Remove

Once the manipulation tactics in your marriage are named and confessed, you can now have a standing agreement to help one another keep your communication clear of each one. It's not easy to lovingly call each other out in the heat of an argument, but at least you're speaking a shared language, having identified a common enemy.

Remember, manipulation has the uncanny ability to quietly sneak itself into otherwise healthy marriages. And if a marriage is already unhealthy, it will only serve to deepen the dysfunction. Fierce wife, be vigilant. Fight for the entire truth, learn to walk in complete transparency, and seek honesty in every facet of your communication. Strive to uproot every manipulation tactic from your marriage and after you've plucked the weeds, enjoy the view as your marital garden begins to flourish anew.

> **KEY TAKEAWAY**
> By learning about your own manipulation habits, you can root them out and walk in new levels of truth and love.

MEDIOCRITY VS. MASTERY

Mediocrity	*Mastery*
Uses manipulation tactics (knowingly or not) for selfish gain	Seeks to eradicate manipulation tactics from all communication
Doesn't ask for help in revealing blind spots	Earnestly asks God, husband, and other godly women to help identify manipulative tendencies
Refuses to admit when manipulating, won't repent	Recognizes and repents of manipulation

APPLICATION QUESTIONS

As you read through the common manipulation tactics above, did any feel close to home? If so, which ones?

Take an honest inventory of your last few arguments. Did you deploy any manipulation tactics? Write them down along with any "trigger" phrases that help you identify them.

CHAPTER FIVE

The Wholehearted Yes

Whoever restrains his words has knowledge,
and he who has a cool spirit is
a man of understanding.
Proverbs 17:27

Elisabeth Elliot once wrote, "Discipline is the wholehearted yes to the call of God. When I know myself called, summoned, addressed, taken possession of, known, acted upon, I have heard the Master. I put myself gladly, fully, and forever at His disposal, and to whatever He says my answer is yes."[3]

As I read those words, my initial response was "Yes, Lord! Yes!" But the more I thought about and processed what it cost to say yes to God, the more hesitant I became. If you're familiar with Mrs. Elliot's story, then you know the weight of her words. For her, saying yes to God meant being a missionary alongside her husband. Saying yes to God meant waking up one day being a widow, alone, with a young daughter. Saying yes to God meant living among and ministering to the tribe who killed her husband.

---

3. Elisabeth Elliot, *Discipline, The Glad Surrender* (Grand Rapids, MI: Revell, 2006), 16.

For Elisabeth Elliott, saying yes to God came at a great price, and still she obeyed. It makes one wonder, *What am I willing to surrender to say yes to God?* And, *In what ways might my surrender to God change how I respond to my husband, particularly in moments when I'm tempted to do so poorly?*

In the last few chapters we've explored how a godly and loving response from a wife to her husband is vital to preserving marital unity. Improvement in how you communicate is also a reflection of the sanctifying work of the gospel in your marriage. Whether you're changing your communication method (writing a letter) or recognizing the right manner and time to have more productive conversations, whatever you do must start with a heart that is joyfully surrendered to God. A surrendered heart is a disciplined heart the way Elisabeth Elliot envisioned it: "Discipline is the wholehearted *yes* to the call of God."

So, I must ask: Are you joyfully surrendered to God? And does your surrender show in how you communicate with your husband?

OBEDIENCE ON GOD'S TERMS, ESPECIALLY DURING CONFLICT

In the book of Ephesians, Paul directed husbands and wives to love and respond to each other in ways analogous to the gospel. Husbands are to love their wives as Christ loved the church, and wives are to submit to their husbands as if unto Christ (Ephesians 5:22–25). In unique ways, husbands and wives are both called to say yes in obedience to Christ and no in rebellion to their flesh. Men must love; wives must submit. But there's an important catch; the love and submission must be Christ's versions of love and submission, not ours. Just as a husband doesn't get to choose his version of love, a wife isn't free to choose her version of submission.

He must love *like Christ,* and she must submit *as if unto him.* If this grates on you, you too have a flesh nature, and welcome to the club. Still, godly women must grapple with God's vision for wifely submission—even in communication and *especially* during conflict—just as godly men must contend with Christ's prescription for love in the same cases.

This is all much easier said than done, but we must say it if we are to ever do it. Heated moments make it hard to see clearly and act obediently but it's in those tough moments when our obedience matters most.

I've come to think of my own angry moments as a kind of pop quiz for whether I'm walking by the Spirit or in the flesh. As Paul wrote, "But I say, walk by the Spirit, and you will not gratify the desires of the flesh. For the desires of the flesh are against the Spirit, and the desires of the Spirit are against the flesh, for these are opposed to each other, to keep you from doing the things you want to do" (Galatians 5:16–17). If I'm walking according to my flesh, I bear fleshly fruit, namely "fits of anger" as Paul calls them (Galatians 5:19). In contrast, if I'm walking by the Spirit, I'll bear His fruit, including "love, joy, peace, patience, kindness, goodness, faithfulness, gentleness, [and] *self-control"* (Galatians 5:23, emphasis added). So, in trying moments, I get to choose: fits of anger or self-control. Which option sounds better to you?

RESPONDING FIGHTING WITH FAITH: THREE SACRED RS

Fellow wife, there is a lifelong battle raging within you between your flesh and the Spirit. With whom are you walking? Yourself, alone, and in the flesh? Or with the Spirit, in lockstep, and with joyful obedience? However you answer those questions, let's explore three ways to fight in faith, by God's grace, so you might pass your own flesh-Spirit pop quizzes more often than not: respect, restraint, and reset.

Learn to Generously Give Him Respect

The more familiar you become with your husband and his flaws, the harder it might be to respect him through your words and actions. But the Bible instructs us wives to respect our husbands (Ephesians 5:33), and there aren't a whole lot of qualifications to that imperative. Gary Thomas put it like this:

> "While many people fight to *receive* respect, Christian marriage calls us to focus our efforts on *giving* respect. We are called to honor someone even when we know only too well their deepest character flaws. We are called to stretch ourselves, to find out *how* we can learn to respect this person with whom we've become so familiar."[4]

Your respect, even when unmerited, will speak volumes to your husband. During moments of conflict, it can be a means of disarming him and defusing the situation. Responding with respect is one of the primary ways we can walk by the Spirit when our flesh kicks and screams for our attention. I'll cover respect in greater detail in a later chapter.

Learn the Art of Restraint

I used to think that if I didn't say what I was thinking, then I was somehow being dishonest with Ryan or myself. I felt a great sense of injustice if I didn't somehow convey exactly how I felt. If

---

4. Gary Thomas, *Sacred Marriage* (Grand Rapids, MI: Zondervan), 55.

I was angry or annoyed, he needed to know it—nay, he needed to *feel* it. Sadly, that was about as far as my thought went. I failed to consider the affect my tone and words would have on him. I was deceiving myself.

Consider what Solomon wrote in the book of Proverbs, "Whoever *restrains* his words has knowledge, and he who has a cool spirit is a man of understanding" (Proverbs 17:27, emphasis added). Once that verse worked itself into the corners of my heart, I realized that I can be honest with how I'm feeling about a disagreement with my husband while also exercising wisdom through my response. It goes on to say, "Even a fool who keeps silent is considered wise; when he closes his lips, he is deemed intelligent" (Proverbs 17:28). The lesson for wives here is to learn the art of restraint in our words. Even if it feels like you might blow your top, take a breath (perhaps try counting to three in your head; it worked for me) and try to think past the feelings in that tough moment. Ask yourself, *Do I really need to say this?* Or should *I say this?* Or *How will what I say affect him?*

God's Word is true and faithful to guide you through tension-filled moments. Restraint doesn't mean you don't say anything. It simply means that you stop, think, filter, discern, and then respond by the Spirit, not the flesh. Godly restraint is the difference between a wife's flesh-fueled reaction and her Spirit-led response. You will resolve conflicts faster while honoring and respecting your husband by learning and exercising the art of restraint.

Learn to Reset by Repentance

So, what happens when you don't respond with godly restraint? What are you commanded to do when you sin against your husband by responding to him, not in love, but with disrespectful words, tone, or manner?

Fierce wife, there is no quicker, wiser, or better way to reset your heart than through repentance. First to God and then to your husband. Through repentance you acknowledge how you've offended God. It is how you turn from yourself and submit to his authority in in your life.[5] Jesus said his mission was to call sinners to repentance (Luke 5:32) and to save them from their sin (1 Timothy 1:15). And discipline from God is a sign of his love and therefore, an occasion to be celebrated, not resented or despised (Hebrews 12:5–13). Repentance has a unique way of reorienting your heart and realigning your gaze back onto Christ. It is how you mortify your flesh and put on your new self (Ephesians 4:24). Mistakes and sin are inevitable, but God has made a way for you to do an about face and turn back to him to find you have been forgiven, yet again, by your loving, long-suffering, and gracious Savior (Matthew 18:22).

In the moments where you want to fly off the handle and respond without respect or restraint, look to Christ. Ask him for help, then by God's grace, walk with the Spirit. You won't nail it every time, but that's not the point. The point is obedience, if not in the moment of speaking, then in turning back toward Christ soon after. Remember, while emotions feel heavy and urgent, they have a way of passing when we exercise wisdom through restraint. So let them. You need not ignore how you feel or stuff your emotions into oblivion, but as a follower of Christ, you are called to preside over them with Spirit-led self-control as you offer unto God your whole-hearted *yes*.

---

[5]. https://www.gotquestions.org/Bible-repentance.html

KEY TAKEAWAY

A disciplined, restrained response is costly, but its fruit is otherworldly.

MEDIOCRITY VS. MASTERY

Mediocrity	Mastery
Gives respect sparingly, which shows through a lack of restraint	Seeks to apply God's version of submission and respect, even if difficult
Fails or refuses to restrain words because they feel right	Restrains words wisely
Doesn't repent when wrong	Repents quickly when necessary

APPLICATION QUESTIONS

Of the three ways to fight in faith (respect, restraint, reset through repentance), which one would you say you struggle with the most? Why?

Consider these wise words from Elisabeth Elliot: "Discipline is the wholehearted yes to the call of God." What are a few ways you can respond with a wholehearted yes to God through discipline in your communication (or otherwise)?

CHAPTER SIX

Respect is Not a Curse Word

*Wives, submit to your own husbands, as to the Lord…
and let the wife see that she respects her husband.*

Ephesians 5:22, 33

Many Christian marriage books for wives venture to articulate the needs of men. Unsurprisingly, among the first are *always* respect or honor (or both). As the fabled Jimmy Evans plainly states, "Honor is a man's greatest need."[6] I emphatically agree.

Your husband's God-given need for honor, especially from you as his wife, is not something you can ignore and still expect to have a thriving marriage. As I'll explain, honoring your husband is an act of obedience to God that can, and must, be joyfully embraced. This is true especially with your words. Nothing can build up or tear down a man quite like his wife honoring or dishonoring him through her words.

But there's a massive elephant in the room: What if he doesn't *deserve* honor or respect? How can you speak to and treat him how

---

6. Jimmy Evans, *Marriage On the Rock* (Dallas, TX: XO Publishing, 2019),170.

God instructs—especially when he isn't behaving in an honorable or respectful way? These are questions every wife asks to varying degrees at one point or another in her marriage. And how you answer it says much about your views of Christ and Scripture.

To be clear, I'm not talking about situations involving abuse. That is a different conversation requiring a specific path toward healing. Here, I'm talking to the wife who is in a lackluster marriage. She feels as though her husband is undeserving of her respect much or all the time, and as a result, she struggles to honor him. If that's you or has ever been you, this chapter is likely to make you uncomfortable. That's okay. I'm asking you to consider, pray, and ask the Lord how you can fulfill one of your husband's greatest needs *even* and *especially* in those moments when he is unworthy of your honor. Let's do this.

HONOR AND RESPECT ON GOD'S TERMS

The imperatives in the verses for this chapter don't come with qualifiers. "Wives, submit to your own husbands, as to the Lord… and let the wife see that she respects her husband" (Ephesians 5:22, 33). They are often bristling to the wife whose husband isn't acting honorably, but all Christian women who seek to live by God's word must grapple with them. Most of us would love it if those passages read more like, "Submit to your husband, as to the Lord, whenever he proves himself worthy of your submission," and "Let the wife see that she respects her husband whenever he's acting respectably." But alas, they don't read that way. So, you and I have a choice. We can either gloss over (read: ignore) these tough passages and respect our husbands when we feel like they deserve it, or we can learn something new about ourselves and God's way.

To drive the point home, consider the responsibilities Paul placed on husbands which, by the way, no one seems to take issue with, despite how unbalanced they are. He wrote, "Husbands, love your wives as Christ loved the Church and gave himself up for her" (Ephesians. 5:25). No big deal, right? Just love like Jesus, all the time, without exception, even unto death! Just as with Paul's commands to wives, there's no qualifier; but what if husbands pretended there were? What if men functionally acted as though the Bible instructed them to love their wives *only* when they're behaving in a manner worthy of husbandly love? Flipping the script makes the breakdown more obvious? Love can't function that way. Perfection is as unattainable for wives as it is for husbands, and that's precisely the point of marital love operating within the marital covenant. If the commands Paul gave to husbands and wives were contingent on anyone deserving love or honor, no one would be loved or honored most of the time, and what does that get us? A big fat nothing-burger with a side of fried bitterness.

Praise God that he doesn't love us like this! And thank Jesus he doesn't allow his married disciples to love like this either. If he had, marriage would be selfish, hopeless, and ultimately fruitless. And, instead of calling us to an unattainable standard, God initiated the actions *of* love, which empower us to obey his commands *to* love. We can now love because of how he first loved us: sacrificially and unconditionally (2 Peter 1:3). Knowing that God understands the depths of your sin and continues to patiently draw you nearer to him through his love should spur you on in your journey to love, honor, and respect your husband despite his imperfections and unworthiness. We must be mature enough to admit and embrace that Paul's commands to wives are not optional, they're required.

REASONS WIVES DON'T HONOR OR RESPECT THEIR HUSBANDS

To further expose the elephant in the room, below are a few reasons why wives struggle to respect their husbands. Do any of the following sound familiar to you?

He Lacks Maturity

Whether he lacks maturity in general or spiritual maturity, the wife of an immature husband struggles to respect a man who still acts like a boy.

Familiarity

More than anyone else, a wife sees her husband's failures, weaknesses, and inconsistencies. Critical wives will struggle with this more than most since they're quicker to notice faults.

Family of Origin

This wife grew up in a family where Mom "wore the pants" while Dad provided the paycheck and little else. How men and women function in marriage is more informed by her experiences growing up than God's Word.

He is Insecure

This wife's husband hasn't yet stepped into his responsibilities as provider, protector, or leader because he lacks confidence. Though she wants him to step into his potential, his lack of confidence makes it hard for her to respect him until he does.

He Doesn't Lead Spiritually

In many ways, this is a culmination of one or more descriptors from above. This wife finds it hard to respect her husband because historically, he's abdicated spiritual leadership responsibilities in the home. Whether he works long hours, plays too many video games, makes excuses, or just lacks any meaningful opinion, his wife struggles to feel and show respect toward him.

He Lacks Character

This wife's husband has patterns of ongoing, unrepentant sin that may include things such as alcoholism, drug abuse, pornography, or other behaviors that consistently cause problems in their marriage. The dysfunction his sin has caused in their family wearies and embitters his wife. Respecting him is often the last thing on her mind.

She's Arrogant

For whatever reason, this wife believes she is better than her husband, either morally, financially, spiritually, intellectually, or all the above. Her high views of herself make it impossible to have a high view of her husband, even if he's trying to grow and lead.

FROM ATTITUDES TO ACTION

The above list of reasons helps explain why wives struggle to show respect. But each reason highlights corresponding attitudes in her heart that materialize as specific actions. Tangibly speaking, how might a wife's attitudes of disrespect lead her to *act* or *behave* disrespectfully toward her husband?

A wife might show a lack of respect for her husband by:
- Passive aggressively undermining his decisions
- Speaking to him in a condescending tone
- Failing or refusing to prioritize him in daily routines
- Making fun, mocking, or invalidating his sincere efforts
- Complaining continually to him or about him to others
- Flirting with other men either in person or online

- ◆ Withholding intimacy willingly or by refusing to initiate or engage
- ◆ Ignoring his requests or leadership regarding family budget decisions
- ◆ Purposefully manipulating him to get what she wants
- ◆ Nagging (enough said)

It's a dark list, right? I was convicted just by writing it. Did you see yourself, even faintly, in any of the above actions? The good news is that even if you're guilty of many of the above, there's always room to grow. Now, let's look at reasons why a wife can turn from the above behaviors and learn to honor and respect her husband, even if he's less than perfect.

REASONS TO RESPECT YOUR MAN

I want to talk tangibly about reasons you can respect your husband, but first, in the interest of cutting exceptions and "what abouts" off at the pass, let's take a paragraph to discuss how honor, respect, and submission relate to a husband's sin.

Does God's command for wives to respect their husbands mean we must gloss over his sin? Not at all. Does it mean you submit to your husband, no matter what he wants or asks? Not remotely. If your husband asks anything of you that is against God's Word, obey God instead! Christ is your King; your husband is your husband. Always obey your King, and whenever possible, so far as it is up to you, honor Christ by how you respect your husband. Your husband will give an account to God for how he loves you through sacrifice just as you'll give an account for how you love him through respect. So, as far as you're able, obey God and honor your husband, but if forced to choose, honor God. Back to the topic at hand.

As a wife, you have many reasons to respect your husband aside from how he acts. Let's go through a few.

God Says So

Based on what we read in Ephesians, respect is a biblical directive for wives. So, in the very simplest terms, you can respect your husband *because* he's your husband. The simple act itself is a sign of godliness. Simple enough, right?

You're Secure in Christ

In an ideal situation, both husband and wife share an implicit respect for one another. This means both parties actively work both to show and to gain respect in the relationship. As a theme, they share effort and desire, though various habits, but sin might make things seem otherwise. This sharing of desire ebbs and flows, and at times it's uneven. Perhaps you're trying harder than he is, or the opposite is true. Still, you can love and respect one another. For example, what if your husband is arrogant and dismissive in how he speaks to you? Can you still respect him? Yes. You can respect him because you are a child of God, and your identity is secure in Christ. This means your ability to respect your husband does not depend on how he treats you.

But women beware; respect and passivity are not the same. You need not be a doormat! Remember Jesus' words, "Pay attention to yourselves! If your brother sins, rebuke him, and if he repents, forgive him, and if he sins against you seven times in the day, and turns to you seven times, saying, 'I repent,' you must forgive him" (Luke 17:3–4). If needed, it's good and biblical to rebuke a brother when he sins against you. If he recognizes it (godly men will), let him repent, extend forgiveness, and move on. It's possible to do all of this while never acting disrespectfully as a wife. That's not to say it's easy, but only that it's possible. You'll need help, which is the next point.

You Have the Holy Spirit

I'm a firm believer that we take for granted just how active the Holy Spirit is in our daily lives. Marriage is no exception. Just as he convicts of sin, he helps us with the particulars of walking out the righteousness God requires. Consider what Peter wrote,

> *His divine power has granted to us all things that pertain to life and godliness, through the knowledge of him who called us to his own glory and excellence, by which he has granted to us his precious and very great promises, so that through them you may become partakers of the divine nature, having escaped from the corruption that is in the world because of sinful desire. For this very reason, make every effort to supplement your faith with virtue, and virtue with knowledge, and knowledge with self-control, and self-control with steadfastness, and steadfastness with godliness, and godliness with brotherly affection, and brotherly affection with love. For if these qualities are yours and are increasing, they keep you from being ineffective or unfruitful in the knowledge of our Lord Jesus Christ.* (2 Peter 1:3–8)

The divine power Peter wrote about is the Holy Spirit himself who is at work in you, producing his fruit that allows you to partake in the nature of God through otherworldly holiness and love. Even with the power Christ promised (John 14:16–17), you are called to "make every effort to supplement your faith" with virtue, self-control, and godliness (among other things). Why? To "keep you from being ineffective and fruitful." So, sister, the Holy Spirit is alive, well, and active in your life producing real fruit. It's his power that allows you to act obediently to God's word by respecting your husband even when your flesh would quickly have you do otherwise.

WAYS YOU CAN RESPECT HIM

Finally, let's look at tangible ways wives can honor their husbands through communication.

Ask Him

Not sure how to make him feel respected? Ask him. When does he feel most respected and honored in your conversations? When does he feel most disrespected? Why? Be humble and enter the conversation with a soft, grace-filled heart that is ready to listen, discuss, and apply.

Pay Attention to Him

Life, busyness, phones, chores, daily life, children, and more all have one thing in common: though good, they can become constant distractions. As far as you're able, learn to set aside distractions and give your husband your undivided attention at some point every day. This is one of the most potent ways a wife can signal respect without saying a single word.

Support Him Explicitly

Whether he succeeds or fails, support your husband in his work! Be his biggest cheerleader in victory and his closest confidant in failure. Admire him on the mountaintops and encourage him in the valleys. Wherever you are, you're there together.

Express Gratitude Toward Him

Instead of complaining or nagging your husband about what you lack, thank him for what you have, including all he does and who he is. Thank him for what he has provided for you and your family. It may not be perfect provision, but you can still let your gratitude show.

Repent to Him

If you have been disrespectful in how you have spoken to him and/or in how you have spoken about him to others, repent and seek reconciliation. If you never see an occasion to repent to your husband, it says more about your heart than his.

Pray for Him

Finally, if you're struggling with a husband who seems undeserving of respect for whatever reason, begin praying for him daily. Praying for him will bring clarity and humility to your perspective as you present your requests to God, remembering that you're both loved by him.

IF IT WERE EASY, EVERY WOMAN WOULD DO IT

If you take one thing away from this chapter, let it be this: your husband may not be perfect, but your God is. And, God has called you to a standard of honor, respect, and submission that will never make sense if it's based on your husband's merit. So instead, respect your husband out of obedience to God. You know you're loved, and you know you have a Helper; now do as Peter encouraged, "make every effort to supplement your faith with virtue" (2 Peter 1:5). Set aside arrogance and conceit, admit your own need for grace, and extend grace through respect. Doing so means trusting God and refusing to settle for worldly patterns of communication. It's one of the most challenging skills many wives will learn, but it's also one of the most rewarding.

> **KEY TAKEAWAY**
> A wife's manner of communication signals her respect, and the respect a wife has for her husband says more about her than it does him.

MEDIOCRITY VS. MASTERY

Mediocrity	Mastery
Sees respect as a cultural suggestion	Understands respect as a biblical command
Insists that respect must be earned to be given	Gives respect freely and joyfully
Refuses to offer one-sided respect when needed	Speaks honestly without disrespecting

APPLICATION QUESTIONS

In what ways has God's Word shaped your definition of respect?

What are some ways you tend to withhold respect from your husband or actively show him disrespect?

What are two to three tangible ways you can show your husband greater respect?

CHAPTER SEVEN

The Words of a Wife to Her Beloved

My beloved speaks and says to me:
"Arise, my love, my beautiful one, and come away,
for behold, the winter is past;
the rain is over and gone."
Song of Solomon 2:10

There is one topic most couples face with varying degrees of agony, so I thought it worthy of its own chapter. That topic is *sex*. Having been married for almost twenty years, I still blush whenever Ryan and I must talk about *it*, whether it's on the podcast, for an event, or just between us. It's a sensitive topic that requires wisdom and delicacy because it is intimate and soul bearing.

Countless couples write to us about the challenges they face regarding sexual expectations, hopes, desires, frustrations, and even hurts in their marriage. All of it can be difficult to discuss, especially when there might be past sexual experiences or trauma to sort through. While special attention is needed to successfully communicate through such issues, I'd like to go a different direction here.

In this chapter I'd like to discuss how you communicate in an *intimate manner toward your husband* before, during, and even after sex. Specifically, what sorts of sexual phrases, words, allusions, and the like are appropriate and godly for Christian women to say to their Christian husbands? Maybe this is new to you, or maybe it's just been a long time since you've given it any thought—either way, let's dive into Scripture to find all the answers that are available to us.

How might a godly wife speak to her husband *during and about* sex?

THE SONG OF ALL SONGS

According to my husband, "The Song of Songs is a masterclass on intimate communication."[7] Can I get an Amen? The mere fact that this eight-chapter book is part of the Bible is enough to show us the weight of its content. The question of how to speak throughout intimacy is an important one, and talk between lovers, while private, is good to get right. Sensual speech toward one's spouse is blessed by God (as we'll see). And not only does intimacy matter, but how we *communicate intimately* matters as well.

For starters, the title *Song of Songs* highlights the book's place among poetic literature. It is the song of all songs! As one commentator notes, the title could be meant to infer that it is "the very best" of all songs.[8] The Song of Songs is not just a flyover

---

7. Ryan Frederick, *How a Husband Speaks* (Tacoma, WA: Lion Press, 2023), 102.

8. Commentary on Song of Solomon 1:1 from The ESV Study Bible (Wheaton, IL: Crossway, 2008), 1216.

book in the Bible; it's a masterpiece worthy of appreciation and application alike.

SENSUALLY SPEAKING

The interpretation and application of the content may vary, but one thing most agree on is that the Song of Songs is clearly sensual poetry expressing romantic love between a young man and a young woman in marriage. And, though much of the imagery is foreign to our modern minds, make no mistake, the book is quite, I'll say, *spicy*.

Given that, let's look at four themes from the Song of Solomon that show us how spouses might communicate sensually in marriage. Also, please note that my use of the word "erotic" isn't meant to indicate carnality or lust in sensual communication but rather the overtly sexual nature of the themes observed.

Here are four themes from Song of Solomon that tell us something about how to communicate sensually.

1. *Erotic Physical Admiration*

The Song is full of examples of the beloved and her husband complimenting one another's physical appearance. And this isn't just because they're objectively attractive, it's that they are positively attractive *to each other*.

The young man says, "Behold, you are beautiful, my love, behold, you are beautiful!" (Song of Solomon 4:1) Then, he verbally admires her many features from head to toe. Her eyes, hair, neck, lips, and even her breasts are mentioned. Every facet of her body is delightful to him. Finally, as if to throw his hands up in resignation at her perfection, he concludes, "You are altogether beautiful, my love; there is no flaw in you" (Song of Solomon 4:7). She is flawless in his eyes, and he *must* tell her so, and she reciprocates.

In response, the young woman writes, "My beloved is radiant and ruddy, distinguished among ten thousand" (Song of Solomon 5:10). Just as he did, she begins admiring his body, from his head down to column-like legs and back up to his mouth. There is no doubt that this woman thinks her husband is a sexy sight to behold. And (as is the point of this chapter) there is no doubt that *she wants him to know it*. So, she tells him out loud just as he did to her.

At this point it's important to pause and ask yourself, *Is this something my husband and I could do?* Could you admire your husband from his head to his toes and back up again? *Should* you do this? Honestly, it seems like the perfect place to start if this type of conversation feels new or awkward. What do you admire and love about your husband's body? And why? The marriage covenant God's ordained place to express these types of intimate admirations, so even if it's a bit uncomfortable at first, I say go for it!

As readers, we should note that the above verses are not only observations, but they're also admirations *with an erotic end goal in mind*. Both the lover and the beloved are expressing a deep desire to see their emotional love physically consummated in the act of making love. They're anticipating intimacy, which is the next theme we'll explore.

2. Erotic Anticipation

In the Song, both the lover and the beloved desperately crave one another. Their expressions of admiration carry with them full *anticipation* of their sexual appetites being satisfied. They're not content dancing the night away and leaving it at that. They want the dancing to lead where the Baptists said it would. Maybe you're thinking, *Goodness, this sounds wonderful but unattainable. I can't remember the last time my husband and I desired each other like this at the same time.* Take heart, friend. Once again, the Bible provides us with an image of what *can* be experienced in a Christian marriage. It may take some practice and persistence, but it will get easier as things begin to warm up between you through conversations like these.

Back to the Song. The lover and his beloved are sick with anticipation, and it shows in their speech. As the woman says, "I adjure you, O daughters of Jerusalem, if you find my beloved, that you tell him, I am *sick with love*" (Song of Solomon 5:8, emphasis added). Also, "Let my beloved come to his garden, and eat its choicest fruits" (Song of Solomon 4:16). Her love is invitational and she's not content for him to stay at an arm's length. She wants him close, and her speech has made as much clear. She calls herself *his* garden, not just to be admired, but to be tasted and consumed. Like I said, steamy, right?

Of course, the man is not silent either. He says things like, "Your navel is a rounded bowl that never lacks mixed wine, your belly is a heap of wheat," (Song of Solomon 7:2) and "Your stature is like a palm tree, and your breasts are like its clusters. I say I will *climb* the palm tree and *lay hold of its fruit*" and "Oh may your breasts be like clusters of the vine, and the scent of your breath like apples" (Song of Solomon 7:7–8, emphasis added).

Although his terminology may seem odd to us, it's clear that his language is *not* passive or flippant. It's language that describes partaking, enjoying, and experiencing. After all, what would a man of the ancient times do with bowls of mixed wine, heaps of wheat, and clusters of fruit? He would drink deep, have his fill, and delight in every flavorful sensation.

3. Mutual Conversation

The Song of Solomon is a dialogue. *Both* the lover and the beloved are contributing to the conversation. Each person is giving of their words and of themselves. As the young woman says in multiple places, "I am my beloved's, and my beloved is mine" (Song of Solomon 6:3). They've both given themselves over to each other, which is evident even in the *manner* of their back-and-forth exchange.

The takeaway here is that sensual communication is a dance and both partners must participate for it to work. Practically, one spouse may initiate the communication, but it takes two to verbally tango. Otherwise, things can get weird fast. The solution? Have a discussion (or lots) about how sensual communication could function in your relationship. When can it work? When does it most definitely *not* work? What are your expectations as a wife? What sorts of words and phrases will you use? And, what makes you both feel most comfortable *and* aroused? To help with this, let's look at the next theme.

4. The Talk is Edifying

When it comes to bedroom talk, there *is* a line of purity that can be crossed and it's not always clear where it lies. While the language of Song of Solomon is very sensual, it's also pure and decent. The warning here is to steer clear of language that can cheapen sex or degrade one another, as such speech dishonors your husband, pollutes the marriage bed, and dishonors God.

The author of Hebrews wrote, "Marriage is to be held in honor among all, and the marriage bed is to be undefiled" (Hebrews 13:4 NASB). While this passage is referring to things like fornication and adultery, I would argue that the words uttered in the bedroom must be carefully curated as to not *import* defiling practices and fantasies from unholy sources (think R-rated movies, shows with nudity, porn, explicit music, or books). In other words, speak to your husband with the honor and respect that befits both him and your marriage. Ask him to do the same for you. And both of you, speak of sex as the treasure God created it to be. Keep it classy. Don't cheapen the experience; enhance it. Your words don't need to be lewd to have the desired effect.

YOUR TURN

In an ideal marriage, both husband and wife are committed to giving their whole selves over to each other for their whole lives. That's why you're reading this book! You probably want to learn to communicate well with your husband so you can love him better.

Similarly, learning to speak sensually is an opportunity to love your husband (and him, you) in new and profound ways. As we've seen, the Song of Solomon has shown us just how spirited sensual talk can get. I'll leave it up to you and your beloved to take it from here.

> **KEY TAKEAWAY**
>
> The question of how to speak throughout intimacy is an important one, and talk between lovers, while private, is good to get right. Sensual speech toward one's spouse is speech blessed by God.

MEDIOCRITY VS. MASTERY

Mediocrity	*Mastery*
Doesn't value communication during intimacy	Understands the importance of communication throughout intimacy
Avoids talking about sensual speech	Seeks to have candid conversations about what works and doesn't work
Uses sensual speech to self-satisfy	Uses sensual speech to edify her husband

APPLICATION QUESTIONS

Would you say you and your husband feel comfortable speaking sensually to one another before, during, and after sex? Why or why not?

How might being thoughtful about sensual speech improve your intimate life?

As a challenge, I encourage you to set aside an evening soon to talk to your husband about this topic. How might you start that conversation?

CHAPTER EIGHT

To The Pen!

In the beginning was the Word,
and the Word was with God,
and the Word was God.
John 1:1

I felt so grown up the day I received my first diary. I was just a little girl, but I remember it clearly. It had a lock on the side with a key you could safely hide away. The diary was a sage green color with a picture of a princess riding a unicorn on the front. I was told that this diary was a place for me to write down all my thoughts, dreams, fears, prayers, or anything else I desired and no one would ever read it unless I let them, since I alone held the key. I think that's about when I began to grasp the unique power and opportunity for written words to capture and communicate thoughts (though I would have never said it that way). Still, the idea of writing to encapsulate and keep the things I felt was exciting. Thus began my ambitions to be a writer.

Starting then, any free moment I had was spent writing in my journal. I'd even ask to go to the library to check out more books to read so I could write about them. I carried these childhood memories into my future, and now our family is, as my husband will tell you, a family where books are life. And quite literally! Books like this one are the way our family carves out a living, and books written by others are how we grow, educate, and disciple our children. And of course The Book, shows us the path toward salvation and abundant life in Christ here on earth. Writing in that small diary helped me discover that books and writing were true treasures to my young soul. They still are.

HAS THIS CAPULET MET HER MONTAGUE?

Now, fast forward to the fall of my sophomore year in high school. Providentially, I was enrolled in an English class with this boy named Ryan Frederick. Though he had started at our school the previous year, we ran with different crowds, so we had very little interaction. I rolled with the "good" kids, while he was a product of '90s Seattle Grunge. I liked TLC and the Dixie Chicks, and he preferred Pearl Jam. I sang church songs while he strummed Nirvana tunes on his Stratocaster. If you know the era, you get the picture. So, though I knew about Ryan, we had little reason to interact, until English class.

I don't remember what we were reading or discussing, but I *do* remember the first time I *noticed* Ryan, and I discovered that I very much wanted him to notice me back.

It was a blustery fall day when I realized that my previous assumptions about him might have been wrong. Our teacher asked a question and Ryan raised his hand to answer. I was stunned by his thoughtful, precise response. I don't remember his words exactly, but I clearly remember how they made me feel. He was articulate and he used words that were beyond a high schooler's vocabulary. Honestly, he blew my mind and I remember thinking, *Who is this guy, brilliantly answering questions about the last few chapters we read? I didn't even know he liked to read.* Ok, I'm not trying to sound harsh, but I was clearly clueless about him.

I became smitten that day in Mrs. McCrady's English class. I could tell he loved words. I loved words. We were perfect for each other! Did I mention his mom also taught English Literature? Swoon! (Also, that explained things a bit.) From then on, I *had* to get to know this guy. Apparently, he had "liked" me the first time he saw me more than a year before, but he thought I was too good for him. I didn't know this until after we began dating,

With a few weeks of English classes our friendship grew. As high schoolers without cell phones did, we began exchanging handwritten notes. We'd pass these notes in the hallway and our relationship began to bloom. I still have a few of the notes from our early relationship and they are among my most valued treasures. There's something uniquely timeless about handwritten words, especially when they come from the man you love.

POWER IN THE PEN

Writing is a wonderful tool that can be wielded for many purposes. It can be a marker of time, like the notes we exchanged in our youth, a marriage journal, or writing letters to each other on anniversaries, birthdates, and special occasions. Writing can also be a way to process difficult seasons and happenings in a healthy way or a means to encourage and uplift one another in marriage. While I'm an advocate of handwritten notes, I believe every form of written words can be productive to this end.

Fierce wife, if you find yourself struggling to adequately communicate your love to your husband, or if you are unable to articulate your feelings of hurt, fear, or frustration around a sensitive topic, might I suggest writing? You can write for your own benefit, for his, or for the benefit of your union. Whatever your objective, writing is a uniquely powerful and productive way to process feelings and emotions. As we have discovered in our marriage, handwritten letters serve at least three functions:

Function #1: Productively Venting Through Rough First Drafts

Whenever we've had to deal with a deep, frustrating, or ongoing conflict in our marriage, we've found that writing out our feelings—the good, the bad, and the ugly—gives us a safe place to vent. The key here is that we'd write them knowing we wouldn't necessarily share them with each other. This isn't because we're hiding or keeping secrets, and it certainly isn't because we were berating or dishonoring each other through undisclosed rants. Instead, it's because the purpose of the letters is to process and vent productively about the situation to communicate more effectively later.

By venting productively, I mean acknowledging your feelings, but submitting them before the Lord. It's a "taking captive every thought and making it obedient to Christ" (2 Corinthians 10:5) kind of productivity. This contrasts with venting *unproductively*, which would involve complaining and grumbling and refusing to acknowledge God's provision and goodness, despite the present circumstance. Just read the first few verses Numbers 11 to see how God responded to unrestrained Israelite complaints. Definitely not recommended.

Although you may feel frustration toward your husband and want to complain to God about him, instead kneel before the Lord.

Ask God for clarity and write down questions, flustered emotions, and hurts—but do so as if unto the Lord. This changes your heart orientation and approach right from the beginning. Remember, you are a new creation in Christ. New creations will now battle communication conflicts differently than the old. Again, this isn't an occasion to dishonor or bash your husband and it's never a good idea to shake your emotional fists at God. Job's wife is no example to follow (Job 2:9).

Instead, letters like these allow you to safely articulate what you're feeling so you can get to the bottom of whatever the heart issue is. It gives you time and mental space to think and reflect with Scripture close by, so that you might untangle the rat's nest and begin re-balling the yarn, all before uttering a single word.

Function #2: Responding to Tough Situations and Organizing Emotions

Writing a letter in response to a tough situation helps provide clarity to both the writer and the receiver. A letter is an unthreatening way for you to record and process your thoughts in an organized and thoughtful manner. Personally, doing this has allowed us to deal with the hard aspects of many complex situations, like extended family frustrations, work tensions, relocation, and trauma all without getting lost in our emotions.

Don't get me wrong; many emotions are good and even hardwired by God into the human condition but getting lost in emotions is rarely a good thing. There are many instances where we tried to discuss a touchy topic, but we were quickly caught up in the minutiae, feelings, and the complexities of whatever the topic might be. Writing as a way of processing, responding, and organizing emotions may be the nudge you need to get over communication hurdles that are slowing you down or even halting communication progress altogether.

Function #3: Communicating Affection

As our high school relationship bloomed, Ryan and I began writing more exclusive notes to each other. After we officially began dating, we enjoyed a little more freedom with our feelings and fears regarding the opportunities for sexual impurity our dating relationship created. The letters back then consisted of encouraging each other in our walk with Jesus (so holy, I know). Often, he would also enclose a few heart-dropping compliments toward me as our young love grew. Even as a grown woman, thinking back to those first months and years of dating makes my heart flutter.

Here's the thing, you don't have to be in high school to enjoy love notes with your husband, and you don't have to be newly dating or married to get twitterpated occasionally. He is *your* husband, and you are *his* wife! You alone have exclusive rights to send and receive love letters between you. So take advantage of this unique benefit! Use those letters to not only express your love and appreciation for him, but also to encourage him in the only way a wife can.

GOD AND HIS WORD

Of all the ways God could have communicated his love for us, he gave us the gifts of his Word—Scripture and the living Word, Christ himself. As the verse at the beginning of this chapter says, "In the beginning was the Word, and the Word was with God, and the Word was God" (John 1:1). Whereas the written words of Scripture show us God's will and decree, the living Word is their maximal fulfillment and proof of God's gracious love. In a later letter, John writes, "By this we know love, that he laid down his life for us" (1 John 3:16). There is no better news than the gospel and if God chose the written word for us to know and experience him, we can believe that there is profound value and purpose in the communicative process of writing. Even and especially in marriage.

Friend, love letter or otherwise, when was the last time you wrote to your husband? Maybe it sounds silly and old fashioned, but I'd bet it will touch his heart in fresh and profound ways. Does he know how much you love, respect, and admire him? Have you told him lately how grateful you are for him and for how he loves and serves your family? Wives, we can put wind in the sails of our husbands' hearts by finding the words to tell them how grateful we are for them and express how much of a gift they are from God. And if writing a love letter feels less than timely, consider how a written letter might unjam your communication through whatever you're facing.

If you can, take some time in the coming week to write your husband a love letter. Encourage him with words of your wifely affection. Both of you are likely to be delighted and surprised, and your marriage will be built up for the glory of God.

> **KEY TAKEAWAY**
>
> The written word provides a unique opportunity for communication, be it for breakthrough or to express your loving affection.

MEDIOCRITY VS. MASTERY

Mediocrity	*Mastery*
Vents unproductively through ranting, complaining, or nagging	Takes time to process emotions and communicate them productively
Doesn't value the opportunity available through written communication	Understands the power and place for written communication in marriage
Sees writing as impossible or too difficult to try	Is willing to write if necessary to clear up communication

APPLICATION QUESTIONS

In general, do you consider yourself a clear communicator? Why or why not?

How might writing help you clarify your thoughts and improve your communication with your husband?

How would it make you feel if your husband wrote you an unexpected love letter? How might writing your husband a love letter make him feel loved, even beyond the words you use to write it?

CHAPTER NINE

Learning the Language of Gratitude

*Do all things without grumbling or disputing, that
you may be blameless and innocent, children of
God without blemish in the midst of a crooked and
twisted generation, among whom you shine
as lights in the world.*
Philippians 2:14–15

*The Lord will fight for you,
and you have only to be silent.*
Exodus 14:14

Somehow, as a twenty-year-old I knew that if I married Ryan our life would be full of adventure. In fact, I was banking on it! Little did I know that these "adventures" would require more grit, faith, and endurance from me than I was ready to give.

As a young, somewhat naive bride, all I could dream about was traveling, starting a career, and having just the right (though unknown) number of babies. Our dreams were nebulous and untested, but they were there. When we got married, we were still in college, so our immediate future was pretty cut and dry: finish school. And after that, who knows? Details were unimportant. We were living on love, Ryan's meager janitorial salary, my barista gig, and lots of prayer! Not in that order.

Fast forward about ten years to when our eldest daughter was born. Dela (short for Adelaide) arrived healthy and beautiful about a week before her due date. There is something extraordinary about your first child. Every memory with her was palpable, visceral, and hyper-real. Though we're from the Pacific Northwest, Ryan and I had been living and working in the Southern California desert for five years. About three months after we had Dela, we knew it was time for a transition. We didn't know where we were headed ultimately, but we felt it was time to go home again, regroup for a few months, and go from there. But where?

Since Ryan was a self-employed web developer, we were geographically unbound. We wondered about Northern California, Texas, or even a move overseas. That felt too ambitious. All our family was back in Washington state, and we had many friends back home, but we didn't think it was time to put roots down; at least not quite yet. So, we packed up everything we owned into a twenty-one-foot, *very*-used U-Haul truck we bought for $2,000, stuffed it to the brim, hitched our little car to the back, and threw our bikes on a rack attached to the back of the car. It was a comical sight to behold! Since I didn't want to take our six-month-old baby on the twenty-four-hour road trip from California to Washington, Ryan drove and Dela and I flew. For the record, I was a nervous wreck flying solo for the first time with our baby!

Our plan was to land in Washington, take a few months to get our bearings, then begin exploring other areas where we thought we should live. As Ryan worked from home, I learned what it meant to be a stay-at-home mama, and since we had our sweet daughter who just wanted to be with us—we could go *anywhere*.

Or so we thought.

GRUMBLING AND COMPLAINING 101

I used to wonder how the Israelites could grumble and complain so much toward God after the Exodus. I mean, they had just seen God send ten plagues and deliver them from hopeless slavery! How could they complain against this obviously powerful God who was clearly looking out for them. I soon found out.

One passage that illustrates this happens right before they crossed the Red Sea.

> *When Pharaoh drew near, the people of Israel lifted up their eyes, and behold, the Egyptians were marching after them, and they feared greatly. And the people of Israel cried out to the Lord. They said to Moses, "Is it because there are no graves in Egypt that you have taken us away to die in the wilderness? What have you done to us in bringing us out of Egypt? Is not this what we said to you in Egypt: 'Leave us alone that we may serve the Egyptians'? For it would have been better for us to serve the Egyptians than to die in the wilderness." And Moses said to the people, "Fear not, stand firm, and see the salvation of the Lord, which he will work for you today. For the Egyptians whom you see today, you shall never see*

again. The Lord will fight for you, and you have only to be silent. (Exodus 14:10–14)

Do you hear them? Grumbling, complaining, and throwing their fear-filled anger in Moses' face? They resented Moses for leading them out of familiarity (and slavery) and into the unknown. It seems understandable at first glance, as they were most likely scared for their lives, doubtful of their future, and possibly a bit too focused on themselves. This is where I started to identify with the Israelite journey.

Ryan, Dela, and I weren't necessarily crossing the Red Sea with a slave-driving tyrant and his legion of horse-drawn battle carriages at our backs, but my fear of the unknown was real. We had left our cozy apartment, familiar relationships, and warm weather, for what? This? We were living out of my mom's spare bedroom with everything we owned crammed into an old, ugly, U-Haul truck. I found it impossible not to grumble. I thought, *Has God led us into this wilderness to die?* Dramatic, I know. Ryan and I began to doubt whether God was with us, as we couldn't seem to find our bearings. All the while, just before moving and while still working on websites, Ryan and I were working our "side gig," building this little marriage ministry called Fierce Marriage.

Despite, in hindsight, being right where God wanted us to be, we still felt unsure and uncomfortable. We were groping for handholds in what felt like pitch black darkness.

So, after ruling out Texas, we dreamed about California again (not its politics, but its beauty and warmth). After a quick housing search it was clear that our financial reality was not compatible with Northern California or any part of California, for that matter. Desperate for any place to park the U-Haul, our little family ended up in a fishing town off the coast of Washington state, renting his parent's seaside condo for half its market rate.

Initially it was fun and exciting to finally have a place to land. However, it still wasn't home. We only halfway moved into the condo while the other half of our stuff was still entombed in the moving truck. Westport is a charming coastal town that suffers from chronic economic depression. The locals jokingly call it "a drinking town with a fishing problem." The local grocery store was closed indefinitely because of management issues, so we had to drive thirty minutes each way to Walmart for whatever food and sundries we needed. We were in between seasons, aimless, located hours from all family and friends, and the weather had officially turned into that familiar, perpetual, drizzly Washington gray. This is where the grumbling really set in.

Frustration and bitterness began to take root. Being left alone with our six-month old while Ryan worked at the local coffee shop began to sour my heart. I quietly began to blame him for every ounce of doubt, discomfort, frustration, and uncertainty I felt. In my mind, we were on opposite teams, and I made that clear to him with my words and actions.

I should have listened to Moses, "The Lord will fight for you, and you have only to be silent" (Exodus 14:14) But silence felt impossible. Not when I was this tired, afraid, and without hope.

THE ENEMY OF DISCONTENT

As much as I felt like he was, my husband was not my enemy. Instead, it was the discontentment inside my heart. Discontentment can rear its ugly head no matter what season you're in. Instead of gratefulness for a roof over our heads, I was complaining about how it wasn't a permanent roof. Instead of enjoying the ocean view, I grumbled about not being inland further and closer to our friends. Each day was a battle. *When and how am I supposed to drive the hour round trip needed to get groceries with a baby who hates riding in the car?* First world problems, I know, but it was reality to this new mom.

Thankfully, at the time I was reading Ann Voskamp's book, *One Thousand Gifts,* and it helped identify the source of my struggle as well as how to combat it. She wrote, "Long, I am woman who speaks but one language, the language of the fall—discontentment and self-condemnation, the critical eye and the never satisfied."[9] Ouch! Hearing that truth pierced my heart, but it was exactly what I needed. A critical eye and *never* satisfied…that was me.

So, how would I combat this language of complaining stemming from the deeply rooted discontentment in my heart? How would I fight to keep Jesus at the center of our marriage and full of the life Christ intended for it? As I discovered, the answer was simple: by learning the language of gratitude.

LEARNING A NEW LANGUAGE

Speaking from experience, a complaining wife chips away at the heart of her husband. "A continual dripping on a rainy day and a quarrelsome wife are alike" (Proverbs 27:15). She doesn't motivate or bless him. She doubts, nags, pokes, and prods until he's so raw he either gives up or lashes out. The other proverb is also true, "It is better to live in a desert land than with a quarrelsome and fretful woman" (Proverbs 21:19). Without a doubt, complaining falls under these terms, and I'm sure Ryan had moments when he would have loved to move back to the desert alone!

---

9. Ann Voskamp, *One Thousand Gifts* (Grand Rapids, MI: Zondervan, 2011), 46.

As I've come to realize and grow through, by God's grace, is that complaining is one of my go-to reactions to stress, uncertainty, and discomfort. I've also learned how my verbal vomit and persistent unfiltered processing affects my husband in deep ways. When I complain, my husband hears me doubt not only God's provision, but his as well. A "small complaint" from a wife can quickly be translated by her husband to sound like,

- I don't appreciate you or what you do for our family.
- You're not leading us well (and I could do better).
- What you're doing is not enough. You're not enough.
- I don't trust you or God to take care of us.
- Do you really love us like you say you do?

I'd never purposefully say those things, but those were the signals I was sending: signals of contempt, discontentment, and division.

Fierce wife, if your words are anything like mine during unsure seasons, it's time to learn a new language. Perhaps you could benefit from learning from the language Ann Voskamp calls *eucharisteo* (Greek; meaning to be grateful, to be thankful, to give thanks). For some, this may be the very battle God is asking us to fight to save our marriage: to *learn* the language of thankfulness.

That is the secret to finding the joy and contentment Paul writes about in his letter to the Philippians,

Not that I am speaking of being in need, for I have learned in whatever situation I am to be content. I know how to be brought low, and I know how to abound. In any and every circumstance, I have learned the secret of facing plenty and hunger, abundance and need. I can do all things through him who strengthens me. (Philippians 4:11–13)

In other words, Paul learned how to be content during times of plenty and times of lack (he was in prison!). Finding things to be grateful for in difficult, trying, and unknown seasons is not something we do by our own strength, but it happens by looking to Christ and being satisfied in Him.

FIGHT THE ENEMY AND FIGHT TO WIN

Learning the language of *eucharisteo* is a skill to be cultivated and I'll gladly admit, it's worth every ounce of effort. Consider listing out reasons why you're grateful for your husband and why you thank God for him daily. Consider counting the ways God has provided for you currently and in the past. Think about times when God has touched your heart or answered your prayers. The more you practice being thankful, the more you will grow in your ability to *see* all that God has given you and the gratefulness will multiply. No matter if you are in plenty, in between, or in lack—you can be thankful!

The sneakiest enemies attack from within. You're fighting a real, sneaky enemy who would love to see your marriage destroyed through you being a complaining, grumbling, discontented wife. Instead, cultivate Christ-centered habits of thankfulness that find safety in his grip, contentment with his provision, and certainty in his sovereign will.

KEY TAKEAWAY

Replace complaining and grumbling sincere gratitude, then let that transform how you communicate to your husband.

MEDIOCRITY VS. MASTERY

Mediocrity	*Mastery*
Grumbles without awareness or restraint	Recognizes grumbling and complaining
Takes opportunities for gratitude for granted	Creates habits for gratitude, even for common things
Remains entrenched in patterns of complaining, grumbling speech	Learns to reorient a complaining heart toward gratitude

APPLICATION QUESTIONS

Do you find yourself grumbling and complaining when you face difficulty, discomfort, or uncertainty? If so, recall the most recent instance. How could you turn your grumbling into gratitude next time?

Part of building a habit of gratitude in your daily life means identifying ways to be reminded to be thankful. What are a few routine triggers that could remind you to express conscious gratitude to God and your husband? (Examples include, being in the shower, taking your first sip of coffee, or having your first bite of lunch.)

What are five tangible reasons you're thankful for your husband? Write them below. When you can, read them aloud to him.

CHAPTER TEN

Hangry and Tired?

> *Know this, my beloved brothers: let every person be quick to hear, slow to speak, slow to anger; for the anger of man does not produce the righteousness of God.*
> *James 1:19*

Ryan and I have reached the point in our lives when we have been together longer than we have been apart. We met in high school, dated for two years, and share the sweet memory of graduating together. In fact, one not-so-sweet memory that can still get my blood boiling is from the night of our graduation.

After we took all the pictures, had all the ceremonies, and gave all the hugs, it was time to party. For our school, that meant Senior Night, which was a tradition consisting of all-night events, starting at the end of the graduation ceremony and lasting until 8:00 the next morning. We had no idea exactly what to expect, but since it was planned by senior class parents at a Christian high school, we knew it would be memorable but not too crazy.

After a few festive stops, we ended the night at an indoor sports complex with basketball courts, arcade games, batting cages, and a new game called Spike-Ball (no, it's not the yard game college kids play nowadays). This original version of Spike-Ball was a fusion of volleyball and basketball on a massive trampoline. Imagine a rectangular box with a trampoline for a floor and no roof. Inside, the trampoline floor is divided into two sides by a cushioned wall with a net along the top.

Now, imagine two basketball hoops on both sides. Each player bounces on their respective side, trying either to spike the volleyball and hit their opponent's floor (scoring a point) or make a basket without it getting rejected (scoring two points). First to score twenty-one points wins. Victory depends on aggressiveness, coordinating bounces to your greatest advantage, and the ability to defy physics by changing directions in midair.

By the time we got to the sports complex it was 5:00 in the morning, and we had been partying all night. Ryan and I were both exhausted but too excited to notice; emotions of all kinds ran high. As teenagers, Ryan and I were *slightly* competitive, and it was beginning to show.

As an adult looking back, I realize that night was absolutely a recipe for an argument. But as a senior in high school you don't think about things like hunger and exhaustion; you just go as hard as you can for as long as your body allows. Then, at some point you crash in bed and repeat it all the next day. On this night, there would be a crash for sure. Well, more like a smash.

SO SMUG

A few minutes after we arrived at the sports complex, Ryan invited me to play Spike-Ball. I was completely exhausted, famished, and emotionally raw. To me, it seemed like a good opportunity to get the blood flowing and blow off a little steam. Reluctantly, I hopped up on the trampoline, zipped the net shut, and we began to bounce.

As we played, we laughed and joked. Then, the joking turned into provoking, and I wasn't going to have it. So I started playing as hard as I could. Spiking, bouncing, blocking, jumping, and doing anything I could to win points against my infuriating boyfriend. Ryan, just as adamant about winning, began to escalate his efforts as well. Then it happened.

Seemingly out of nowhere (I still hold him accountable for this), with all the might a high school football player can muster, Ryan smacked the ball as hard as he could. Well, by that point, our bounces had synced, and we happened to be at the same elevation, looking at each other face-to-face over the net. Then yes, you guessed it, the super-sonic Spike-Ball hit me square in the face. All I saw were stars.

Instantly I dropped onto my side on the trampoline, grabbing my face, crying. I fully expected to be bleeding all over myself. Irate, I screamed at him, "What the heck was that for?!" Ryan apologized profusely. He didn't intend to hit the ball directly at me, regardless of the result. He ran to get some ice and a few towels.

Thankfully, there was no blood at all, and my face was barely red. The damage was more to my pride than to my face. With the ice applied, my tears dried up (along with my embarrassment), and we began to chuckle about everything. I learned an important lesson that day: don't expect tiffs with Ryan to go well late at night, *or* when I'm hungry, *or* when I'm just plain worn out.

This far into our marriage, I can confidently say that there is a time and a place for working out every disagreement. I can also confidently say that it's probably not in a Spike-Ball court. Nor is it likely to be at 5:00 am or whenever you're both exhausted. Still, there is a right time and place for every difficult conversation. The tough part is learning to discern where and when, which starts with admitting your limits.

READ THE SIGNS; ADMIT YOUR LIMITS

Understanding your personal and marital limitations is a step toward wisdom. Neither of you are mentally nor emotionally inexhaustible. And, even if you're both determined to handle a tough situation while depleted, it's entirely possible that you'll still bungle it because you're off your game. So, know and admit your limits.

When are you most likely to be hungry, tired, angry, frustrated, or emotionally exhausted? After a long day with the kids? When you're drained after being with large groups of people? Perhaps before stressful events? Late at night? During prolonged times of disconnection from your husband, intimately or otherwise? You name it. As you survey your life, you'll see trends emerge that tell you something about your limitations. Those same trends can often be traced to themes of recurring marital dysfunction.

Knowing and admitting their limits enables wives to do four things better:

1. Discern and avoid inopportune moments,
2. Patiently navigate difficult conversations,
3. Confidently set the stage for communication success,
4. Love your husband better by learning to call timeout for the both of you.

I'm not saying circumstances must be *perfect* for you to have *perfect* communication. It is certainly possible to power through hunger, tiredness, frustration, or impatience in the name of finding quick resolution; but your efforts will be less productive, and results may vary.

So, how might a wife read the signs? See the signs by admitting your limits both mentally and physically. Acknowledge your limits and talk through them with your husband. Then learn to preemptively recognize patterns that lead to limitation-induced communication dysfunction.

RECOGNIZE PATTERNS. ASK QUESTIONS.

Communicating at our best with each other *can* happen every day. But it's important to assess and evaluate each other's physical and emotional states.

If you see a pattern of *when* you and your spouse tend to have fights, and what it is you mostly fight about—it would be wise to take a step back and ask questions to get clarity.

A good friend once told me that "clarity is kindness," so how can a wife communicate kindness to her husband when she recognizes a dysfunctional pattern between them? Through asking questions that would help each other see why they always struggle at a certain time and with a certain topic.

Here are a few questions to get you started:
- Do we tend to fight at a certain time of the day? Why?
- What is the main contributing factor?
- Is there a clear way to alleviate the tension?
- What new rhythms can we implement to avoid falling back into this pattern of poor communication?

Begin with identifying whether it's a physical factor: are we tired, hangry (hungry and therefore angry), or are we just worn out? It may be that you need to stop and eat something, take a break and go on a walk; or simply go to bed and circle back with each other in the morning.

If there is a deeper issue, it will become clear as you assess and eliminate the physical factors. This is freeing in that you won't be make a big deal out of issues that are, in the grand scheme of things, minor.

> **KEY TAKEAWAY**
>
> Admitting and adjusting according to your limits is vital for healthy communication.

MEDIOCRITY VS. MASTERY

Mediocrity	Mastery
Disregards physiological factors as playing a role in communication	Understands and admits physiological limits
Refuses to postpone difficult or touchy conversations until a better time	Foregoes immediacy in favor of better, more effective communication later
Unable to see, in the moment, how tiredness and blood sugar influence perception, reaction, and response	Able to recognize when tiredness, hunger, or other factors are inhibiting healthy dialogue

APPLICATION QUESTIONS

Recall times when you've had arguments or dysfunctional communication. What physiological factors tend to influence how you hear and respond to your husband?

What circumstances typically lead to your physical depletion? Kids, duties, work schedules, or otherwise? Why?

CHAPTER ELEVEN

The Truth About Lying

*Do not lie to one another, seeing that you have put
off the old self with its practices and have put on the
new self, which is being renewed in knowledge after
the image of its creator.*
Colossians 3:9–10

Let's try a quick thought experiment. What if God was a liar? Think about that for a moment, the implications are as massive as they can be. If God was a liar, there is literally no atom in all creation that wouldn't come into question, let alone our assurance of salvation and the undying truths of Scripture. If God weren't true, nothing is true. But he is true, and he says true things, so here we are!

God values truth because God *is* truth—and it's not as if God somehow conforms to truth, as if what is true were true before he made it so. Truth is derived from God himself. We have truth because God made it so, and it finds its very origin in Him. So, when we see Jesus, who is God in the flesh, go so far as to call himself the truth (John 14:6), we know precisely why. At the root, this is why lying is such an affront to God and an insult to covenantal marriage: lying goes against the very character and nature of God himself. This reality cannot be overexpressed.

So, let's raise a few questions. Do you value truth the way God values truth? And similarly, Do you hate lying as much as God hates it? And how might your love for truth and your hate for deceit change how you communicate in your marriage?

GOD'S TRUTH ABOUT LYING

Before going further, let's root our understanding in what the Bible says about truth and lying:

- God cannot lie (Titus 1:2)
- Lying is contrary to God's nature (Numbers 23:19)
- Lying is a sin (Exodus 20:16)
- God detests dishonest scales (Proverbs 11:1)
- "Lying lips are an abomination to the Lord" (Proverbs 12:22)
- Jesus is full of grace and truth (John 1:14, 17)
- Jesus is *the* truth (John 14:6)
- Jesus is the true one with the key of David (Revelation 3:7)

Just with the above list, it's easy to see how Scripture makes it abundantly clear that lying of any kind is contrary to God's nature. It's an affront to his holiness and rebellion against his decree. These are strong words, but how can we take lightly a topic treated so seriously in Scripture? After all, lying doesn't always seem so black and white, right? It's tempting to dismiss white lies as inconsequential nuisances rather than weighty sins. Sister, don't fall for it! We must be avid tellers of truth because we know Truth himself.

Paul wrote to the early church, "Do not lie to one another, seeing that you have put off the old self with its practices and have put on the new self, which is being renewed in knowledge after the image of its creator" (Colossians 3:9–10). Lying is serious business! It indicates whether you're walking in the flesh or by the Spirit—wearing your "old self" or adoring the new.

As I mentioned above, Jesus said that *he* is the way, the truth, and the life (John 14:6). To be in Christ is to be in truth, but what if, upon honest introspection, we find that we do in fact, lie? As mentioned often in this book, the ways we communicate are neon signs pointing us to look in two directions: to the contents of our heart and to the holiness of Christ. A deceitful tongue reveals simultaneously a deceived heart and an abiding need for the honesty of Christ. This is not about being legalistic, it's about holiness. We aren't saved by telling the truth, but by the Truth himself, which should bear fruit of truth in every aspect of our lives.

So I ask you again, have you lied to your husband? Let's look at some of the unique ways wives might tell lies.

THE LIES OF WIVES

How might wives lie in marriage? In my view, there are three types of lies: white lies, lies of omission, and overt deception. Let's briefly examine each one.

White Lies

White lies involve something thought to be harmless or trivial. The thought is that whether you tell your husband the truth, it won't change the outcome. A wife may tell a white lie to her husband because she thinks the truth might stress him out, and since the outcome is the same, why bother? Another example might be spending money without permission or agreement, even though you know your husband would disapprove. "What he doesn't know won't hurt him."

The truth is that white lies, though seemingly trivial, will still chip away at your unity and trust. It's not worth it.

Lies of Omission

These are lies where you intentionally exclude certain information. I once popped a tire by hitting a parking lot curb because I was driving carelessly. When I came home, I told Ryan that we had a flat tire. At the time I didn't think it relevant to share the *exact* method by which the tire popped, he just needed to know that it needed to be repaired. Being the honest kid my mama raised me to be, I couldn't overtly lie to him, so I just told a half truth. Still, it was eating away at me because though I had rationalized the lie in my mind, I knew I wasn't being truthful. So when Ryan asked why the hubcap was damaged so badly, I 'fessed up. As it turned out, he didn't care as much about the tire as I thought he would. His main concern was why I omitted this information in the first place.

Another example of this might be a wife texting or direct messaging a guy online who happens to be an old friend. When asked who they are messaging, she replies, "Oh, no one. Just an old friend." Technically true, but it is still a lie because she is hiding something. Don't buy the lie that you're technically being honest with your husband if you are omitting pertinent information on purpose. Lying, even by omission, will hurt him and you, erode your trust and unity, and in the long run it will cost you more than you're willing to pay.

Overt Deception

Overt deception includes lies told openly and without regard for truth or consequence. An example of this is when a wife is a compulsive or chronic liar. Typically, this type of lying begins in adolescence. If you have ever experienced being lied to, multiple times, then you will understand the hurt and hopelessness that often goes along with it. Compulsive liars will often employ manipulation tactics (see Chapter) and have other narcissistic traits. They will also tell you that everything is fine when it isn't. They will do their best to hide addiction or an affair or otherwise.

Overt and chronic liars often need outside help. If you struggle with lying in this way, seek help. Talk to your pastor, seek godly, biblical counsel (a pastor will often partner with a godly counselor in cases like these), and do the work it takes to begin walking in truth.

WHAT DISHONESTY DOES

Part of understanding our need for truth is identifying the effects of deception, big and small. Your marriage is a covenant and a promise based on a mutual agreement to love one another truly, faithfully, and for life. Lying directly compromises your covenant. Whether one lies because of insecurity, fear, shame, guilt, or habit, and whatever the occasion, one thing is certain: lying *will* cost you more than you ever wanted to pay.

- I'm often heartbroken by the women who write to us asking for marital help. Habitual deception had devastated her marriage. Almost always, there is a form of deception at the core of whatever issue they're facing. The lies start small and appear to be harmless, but over time, small deceptions develop into fully grown sins and lead to emotional neglect, hidden addictions, out-of-control spending, mounting bitterness, and adultery (both physical and emotional).

Some other effects of lying we've heard from couples include shattered families, stunted communication, flatlined intimacy, trust that seems broken beyond repair, anxiety, and depression. As Paul wrote, "the wages of sin is death," and lying can be heartily counted among the sins he's speaking about. Thankfully, Paul didn't stop there. The whole verse reads like this, "For the wages of sin is death, *but the free gift of God is eternal life in Christ Jesus our Lord.*" (Romans 3:23, emphasis added). Inevitably, ongoing sin chips away at the foundation of every marital covenant until eventually, it's destroyed. Still, we serve a God who is powerful to forgive sin, transform hearts, repair marital foundations, and even transplant teetering marriages onto the bedrock of the gospel. Let's look at the pathway toward truth.

THREE GROUND RULES FOR REAL HONESTY WITH YOUR HUSBAND

Here is the good news: "There is therefore now no condemnation for those who are in Christ Jesus" (Romans 8:1). Fierce wife, your lot is not condemnation, it's freedom! Christ himself said that when you know the truth (which is Christ himself) the truth will set you free (John 8:32). So, live in truth and be free. Walk in the light, be cleansed of sin, and step into enduring fellowship with your husband (1 John 1:7).

Here are three ground rules to get you started down that path. I'm not exaggerating when I say that they revolutionized our marriage.

Honesty Ground Rule 1: Always Tell the Truth

A while back when we were dealing with some deception of our own, we had to work through rebuilding trust and creating clear boundaries. Ryan and I made two promises to one another. The first promise is that either one of us can ask about literally *anything* and the other person will always give a straight, honest answer. It's tempting to downplay sin but doing so minimizes its gravity and increases the chance it will happen again. Instead, commit to stating plainly what sin was committed.

You need not rehash every detail, and as a wife you must resist the temptation to be curious about details, but you do need to state plainly what sin was committed. Choose language like:

I lied to you when I said _____.
I lusted when I thought _____.
I overspent when I bought _____.
I dishonored you by _____.

Whatever the confession, God already knows, and he still loves you. He even died for sinners in the middle of their sin (Romans 5:8). So, speak plainly and honestly, rip off the rotten Band-Aid, and begin to heal.

Honesty Ground Rule 2: Always Love

The second promise we made to each other is that no matter what either of us says in response to being asked, the other will never stop loving them. Neither of you will want to confess when you've made a mistake if you think you're going to get beat up for it. How many times do you sugarcoat sin because you're afraid your husband will withhold his love? Covenant love is stronger than that—it's not easier, but it is stronger.

By clearly committing to truth and love in this way, you give each other permission to bring darkness to light, to walk away from honesty, and step forward into truth. Authentic accountability requires biblical, fierce love. Perhaps that's why Jesus said, "Pay attention to yourselves! If your brother sins, rebuke him, and if he repents, forgive him, and if he sins against you seven times in the day, and turns to you seven times, saying, 'I repent,' you must forgive him" (Luke 17:3–4).

We don't repent just to have our sins thrown in our faces; that's humiliation. Confessing sin always requires *humility*, but never *humiliation*. Christ called sinners to repentance, but he never humiliated them; he forgave. As his ambassadors and followers, we're called to extend the same grace and forgiveness he's shown us (Matthew 18:21–35).

Decide ahead of time that you will love one another no matter what truth comes to light. It doesn't dismiss sin or rid your marriage of consequences, but it does reinforce covenantal love.

Honesty Ground Rule 3: Remove Temptation

The final ground rule is all about boundaries, and good boundaries start with honesty. Be honest with yourselves about what causes sin. Pornography is not a "husband only" battle. If porn is a big issue for you and you always struggle when you're alone at home, time to cut the internet connection (seriously) and get help.

If spending more money than you and your husband have agreed upon is a problem for you, then it's time to destroy the credit cards.

If you're a habitual liar and your online social accounts are causing honesty issues, time to give up the passwords and add some transparency (or better yet, get rid of the accounts altogether). All the above may seem extreme, but sin is serious business. Work together as a team, discuss sources of sin, and create boundaries that reduce or remove temptation from the equation.

THE TRUTH ABOUT LOVE

This is a heavier chapter because lying is a heavy sin. All sin grieves God, but lying has a way of festering in quiet, dark, dank places. Speak up, shed falsehood (Ephesians 4:24), and walk in every ounce of freedom that is yours in Christ. He is a loving God, full of patience and kindness. He is love, and love rejoices with the truth.

KEY TAKEAWAY

God is truth so we must speak truthfully. Lying of any kind undermines trust, communication, and closeness in marriage.

MEDIOCRITY VS. MASTERY

Mediocrity	*Mastery*
Insists that small lies are harmless	Commits to truth telling as paramount for trust and intimacy
Believes some lies are best left unconfessed	Understands that truth is freeing, even if telling the truth is difficult
Fails to establish boundaries around areas of temptation	Works with husband to build boundaries to minimize temptation

APPLICATION QUESTIONS

Ground Rule #1 is to Always Tell the Truth. Have you ever lied to downplay a sin? What fears led you to hide the severity of your sin?

Ground Rule #2 is to Always Love. How might the promise and assurance that you will always be loved help create a more honest communication culture in your marriage?

Ground Rule #3 is to Remove Temptation. What boundaries can you and your husband put in place to remove temptation in your life? Be specific. Consider discussing your boundary ideas (and why you think they're needed) with your husband.

CHAPTER TWELVE

Tongue Taming

> *So also the tongue is a small member,*
> *yet it boasts of great things.*
> *How great a forest is set ablaze by such a small fire!*
> *And the tongue is a fire, a world of unrighteousness.*
> *James 3:5–6*

One of the most perilous periods in a new marriage is the time between the end of the honeymoon phase and the time the couple learns to tame their tongues. The danger comes when you settle into habits in your tone, words, and heart orientation toward your husband that can lead to division between you, hurtful things said, and potentially damaged trust or forfeiture of emotional safety. The tongue is immensely powerful—indeed that's one of my main reasons for writing this book! It's truly capable of bringing life or death. So, as couples continue in marriage, it is paramount that they learn to tame their tongues. But, as James writes, "no human being can tame the tongue" (James 3:8). So, where does this leave us?

Let me invite you back to our first year as a young married couple, when twenty-year-old Ryan and twenty-one-year-old Selena were settling into our new life as the Fredericks. Those first few months were fairly easy and saturated with moments of newlywed bliss. We enjoyed lots of laughter and plenty of happy-go-lucky, married-people activities (you know the ones). Life wasn't easy (we worked and studied a ton), but we experienced very little conflict or frustration between us. It's pleasant and rather easy to be nice and loving toward someone you're still getting to know.

Fast forward a few years and reality set in. My true colors began to show. How I spoke to my husband could have been easily described as sharp, hurtful, argumentative, impatient, and occasionally dismissive. And so you know it was a two-way street, he would say he was short, dismissive, and harsh in ways unbecoming of a godly man.

The devolution of our discourse was leading to discord in every aspect of our marriage. We struggled for consistent intimacy, our homelife felt hurried and tumultuous, our finances grew disunified and riddled with anxiety, and our priorities were bending out of order. Thankfully it didn't take much of this to learn that it wasn't going to work. Our communication tendencies were driving us apart, and isolation was setting in. The untamed communication culture we had amassed was neither glorifying to God nor honoring of each other. Something needed to change, or we were doomed.

BECOMING TWO TRULY AS ONE

Think back to your wedding day. When a couple stands at the altar and says their vows before God and witnesses, they celebrate and eventually leave to consummate their commitment through intimacy. At this point, the two have become one flesh (Genesis 2:24; Mark 10:6–9). There is a marvelous blending of selves and a miraculous mingling of souls that is so mysterious, even the apostle Paul calls the whole ordeal "profound" (Ephesians 5:32). As otherworldly as it all seems, this profound mystery has practical implications for the individuals involved, and Ryan and I were coming to terms with the fine print of marital covenant making.

Among other discoveries, one of our most momentous realizations was that our marital *oneness* meant that we no longer had the freedom to say whatever we wanted, however or whenever we wanted to say it. (For some this is obvious; for us, not so much.) We were young and inexperienced. We lacked wisdom and nuance in how we spoke and the things we said. It was a challenging season for us because neither of us realized how quickly our words would set fire to our unity. When the newness of married life wears off and your old selves settle in, you must learn to fight harder and harder for oneness. Husbands face unique challenges to this end and every wife will have her own set of challenges as well: letting her emotions run the show, using a disrespectful or emasculating tone, complaining and grumbling about what she doesn't have, or arguing to get what she wants, just to name a few.

Choosing to let your tongue run amok, setting fire haphazardly, and starting wildfires will cause more damage than you ever intended in the forms of disrespecting your husband and dishonoring the Lord. Take it from me, firsthand. Thankfully, James has wisdom for us.

JAMES AND THE BLAZE

Take a minute to grab your Bible and read through James 3:1–12. As you may have noticed, James makes a few key points about the tongue.

- ♦ The tongue is small but powerful. (vs. 5)
- ♦ It can set a forest ablaze. (vs. 5)

- "And the tongue is a fire, a world of unrighteousness." (vs. 6)
- It is a part of the body and can set on fire the entire course of your life. (vs. 6)
- It is set on fire by hell. (vs. 6)[10]
- The tongue is untamable by man. (7)
- Full of restless evil and deadly poison. (vs. 8)
- The tongue is God-given, but we use it to curse others made in his likeness. (vs. 9)

Those are no uncertain terms. The tongue is powerful, and its fruit is telling. If you recall, it was also James who wrote, "Show me your faith apart from your works, and I will show you my faith by my works" (James 2:18). James also says that faith without works is dead because faith—if genuine—will by necessity produce good works from the inside out. To be clear, Scripture doesn't teach that we must earn our salvation through good works, and that's not what James is teaching here (see Ephesians 2:5, 9–10).

Similarly, James addresses the potency and danger of the tongue because how one uses it says much about what is in their heart (James 3:10–12). It is an outside-in indicator of holiness. And not only that, but he's also warning hearers of the dangers of a heart that spews forth flames from the tongue. To illustrate this, my husband uses the image of someone walking through a forest with a drip torch,[11] having forgotten to extinguish its flame. Soon, every tree is lit, and the entire forest is going up in flames. The heart

---

10. God created the tongue for good, but the Enemy has corrupted it, thus perverting it for evil. - More info: https://www.gotquestions.org/the-tongue-is-a-fire.html

11. A drip torch is a tool foresters use to drip lit fuel onto the forest floor to perform controlled burns during forest management activities.

provides the fuel, and the tongue is a fire; we'd be wise to tend to both with caution and care.

Still, the same passage tells us that no man—or woman—can tame the tongue. What are we supposed to do? Great question!

You've already answered the first part. If no man or woman can tame the tongue, that means only God can. Our first response is to run *to* God and remember his Word. The Bible teaches that the *same* Spirit that raised Christ from the dead is alive in us today! (Romans 8:11) It is the power of the resurrected Christ and the Holy Spirit within us that enables us to resist and fight off sin, as well as produce the Holy Spirit fruit of self-control.

Fighting sin and resisting the devil is not easy, but it is part of the believer's life. "Submit yourselves therefore to God. Resist the devil, and he will flee from you" (James 4:7). Hold onto that promise and draw near to God. When impatience or frustration begin to bubble up in your heart and you're about to say something you know will only bring damage rather than reconciliation—stop. Resist the temptation, submit to God's Word, apply wisdom, and trust that you can respond in the way he desires.

A WIFE'S UNTAMED TONGUE

Sometimes the best defense against untamed speech is simply recognizing what it looks like, so let's have a look.

A wife with an untamed tongue:

- is sharp or cutting in her responses
- uses her tongue to undermine or destroy her husband's headship
- gossips and complains about her husband to friends
- puts her husband down or degrades him by comparing him to other men

- ignores her husband when she could be encouraging and uplifting him
- is sarcastic
- embarrasses her husband by exposing a flaw to make herself look better

Neither you nor I want to be that type of wife. Flip a few pages back and review the list of attributes of a God-fearing woman described in Proverbs 31. You will find that an untamed tongue is not on the list. A godly wife is one who uses wisdom when speaking to her husband. She has a healthy fear of the Lord and uses her words for the good of her King, her husband, and her household. The words of a wife whose tongue has been tamed by the Lord are indicators of her genuine faith.

THE IMPORTANCE OF TAMING YOUR TONGUE

Sister, God cares about the way we speak to our husbands and, how we speak to them reveals much about our hearts. Have bitterness, rage, anger, frustration, and selfishness welled up within you? Or does your heart overflow with joy, goodness, kindness, holiness, and love? Whatever's inside of you has a way of working its way out through the things we say.

Too much is at stake to let an unbridled tongue run amok. Listen to the words coming from your mouth. Watch your tongue like the barometer for your heart it is. When the tongue is bitter, seek the sweetness of Christ. Control your tongue but look to Christ in every syllable. Ask for heart renewal, so that by God's grace and with the Holy Spirit's help, your tongue might be tamed and used for love and nothing else.

> **KEY TAKEAWAY**
>
> The tongue is sharp and powerful; use yours as a tool and not as a weapon.

MEDIOCRITY VS. MASTERY

Mediocrity	*Mastery*
Doesn't realize the power of her tongue	Understands how powerful the tongue can be
Has an untamed, unbridled tongue	Uses her tongue with great wisdom and care
Uses her tongue to bring death	Uses her tongue to bring life

APPLICATION QUESTIONS

Have you struggled to tame your tongue in your marriage? Why or why not?

Assuming you've struggled with taming your tongue at one point or another, what does an untamed tongue typically look like for you? (Sharp tones, disrespectful words, etc.) What would be the opposite of an untamed tongue in each example?

Specifically, how can you prepare your heart and mind today to rely on the Holy Spirit the next time you're tempted to let your tongue run off untamed?

CHAPTER THIRTEEN

More Than A Meal

Jesus said to them, "I am the bread of life; whoever comes to me shall not hunger, and whoever believes in me shall never thirst."
John 6:35

The following may come across as old fashioned but bear with me. Think about the moments when your husband walks in from his job feeling distraught, overwhelmed, frustrated, and tired. How would he feel if he smelled the aroma of his favorite dinner filling your home and saw a plate of delicious cookies, freshly baked, waiting on the table for him? Is there anything he especially loves that tells him he is valued and appreciated? It's not about the meal itself, but a well-timed meal is a doorway to so many benefits when it comes to communication.

A meal can feed his soul. A meal could be a way of breaking that communication cold snap you've experienced the past few months. Sometimes actions speak louder than words—especially when words are hard to come by. Through the action of making him a meal, you're telling him: *I see you. I love you. I am grateful for you.*

WHAT CAN A MEAL COMMUNICATE?

What could a meal *say* to your husband? In our other work we talk a lot about how one spouse has a direct line of communication to the other spouse's heart. This means *you* have an exclusive line to your husband's heart. He hears you differently than he hears anyone else; your words and actions carry more weight. How are you using this direct line? For your benefit or for his? Fierce wife, never underestimate the affects your words or *actions* have on your husband.

Up to this point we have discussed communication in terms of words. In this chapter, let's examine what your *actions* have to do with communication. In other words, what are you communicating to your husband through your gestures? More specifically when it comes to cooking a meal. In my experience, many wives have left this communication tool unused for far too long. It's time to dust it off and pull it out of our arsenal.

SCRIPTURE + MEALS

Scripture draws attention to food and meals, and the purposes of them. In the Old Testament we see the Jewish calendar and the various Feasts they held. There are also meals that were prepared for celebrations such as weddings. Food was also a form of the recognition of God being Provider (think manna and quail) and our utter dependence on him to be so.

In the New Testament, Jesus multiplied food for large crowds of people who he had been teaching—affirming who he is (Son of God) and his power. In Mark 8:1–10, Jesus feeds a crowd of four thousand, and there are six things he does that we should take note of when it comes to communication. Let's take a look.

"In those days, when again a great crowd had gathered, and they had nothing to eat, he called his disciples to him and said to them, 'I have compassion on the crowd, because they have been with me now three days and have nothing to eat. And if I send them away hungry to their homes, they will faint on the way. And some of them have come from afar.'"

Clearly, Jesus had been teaching the crowd for three days while they with nothing to eat. Though he had fed their souls, he was aware of their physical needs. So, reading on, Jesus broke the bread, gave thanks, blessed a few small fish, and had his disciples pass out the food. And everyone ate until they were satisfied (v.8).

How does Jesus model loving communication? How does he *show* that he cares for the crowd, beyond what he says? There is an ordering of priorities being modeled here by Jesus. And he understands our humanity and finitude more than we ever will. In his full understanding he responds with perfect compassion.

Six Ways Jesus Models Loving Communication

1. *Jesus had compassion on the crowd.* Contrast his compassionate response to one of being irritable, tired, or frustrated. Jesus had every right to *not* be compassionate, but he was.
2. *He knew they were tired.* Jesus understood their physical limits.
3. *He knew they were hungry.* Jesus understood their physical needs.
4. *Jesus was present.* He was physically present with them; he didn't leave them in their time of need.

5. *Jesus gave thanks to the Father.* Jesus prayed *while* he acted to meet their needs.
6. *Jesus multiplied the provision.* Jesus did what only he could do. He multiplied what he provided.

OPEN THE DOOR OF COMMUNICATION WITH A MEAL IN HAND

Could a thoughtful and timely meal communicate compassion, love, and gratitude to your husband? Open the door to his heart with a meal! Follow Jesus' lead:

- **Have compassion for your husband.** The next time he walks in from a long day at work, and you know he's been feeling defeated mentally and spiritually, welcome him with a warm meal and a reassuring hug. Begin the conversation without words. *Show* him you understand and empathize with him. Compassion is disarming to a weary soul.

- **Break cold snaps with warm meals.** A "cold snap" is defined as *a sudden, brief spell of cold weather*. Things get icy in marriage when bitterness builds up from being hurt, mistreated, or misunderstood over a long period of time. Cold snaps happen when we don't nip communication issues in the bud. Cold snaps often leave a couple hungry and tired. Break the cold snap! Begin with a warm meal. At minimum it will feed him. It has the potential to reinvigorate your communication.

- **Be present.** Meals bring people together. As a couple, it is important to come together at the table (figuratively and literally). Being present and not distracted or absent communicates to your husband that he is a priority; that he is valued and worth your time and energy.

- **Give thanks for God's provision.** Being together and taking a moment to give thanks to God for his continued provision has a way of lifting your eyes as well as your hearts. Grumbling and complaining are absent from souls that are filled with gratitude. If discontentment or complaining have become regular guests at your table, kick them out! Stir your affections for the Lord. He is faithful and unchanging (Hebrews 13:8).

MORE THAN A MEAL

As you prepare a meal for your husband, prayerfully consider how this meal can be an opportunity to improve your communication with him.

If this is something that ruffles your feathers or takes you out of your comfort zone, don't worry! It won't always be uncomfortable; in fact, the more you practice serving and loving your husband in various ways, the more joyful it becomes. Again, love always has a multiplying effect.

Fierce wife, trust that being considerate and thoughtful toward your husband by making a special meal is about so much more than making the meal—it's an opportunity for you to love him as Christ loves you. It's a chance to let go of any pride or frustration that might hinder you from coming to the table with a meal, ready to talk. Pray and petition for the Lord to soften your hearts toward one another. Ask him to bring unity between you and your husband. Give thanks to God for your union and celebrate his goodness in your lives.

Rest and remember that the meal is both a door and a place. A warm meal has the potential to open the door for deeper communication while it's also the *place* where communication can thrive.

> **KEY TAKEAWAY**
> Preparing a thoughtful meal for your husband is a unique opportunity to love him with the love Christ has modeled.

MEDIOCRITY VS. MASTERY

Mediocrity	*Mastery*
Sees this type of service as antiquated or beneath her	Serves with warmth, joy, and gladness
Expects her husband to deal with work struggles on his own	Recognizes her husband's work struggles and responds with confident compassion
Doesn't prioritize planning or preparing a meal	Anticipates with excitement the connection and joy possible during a meal

APPLICATION QUESTIONS

What might it mean for your husband if you planned and prepared a special meal solely aimed at connecting more deeply with him? How do you think he would react?

Is there a part of you that bristles against this idea of preparing a meal for this purpose? Why do you think that is?

CHAPTER FOURTEEN

Communication Ruts and Tendencies

So don't be ashamed of the testimony about our Lord, or of me his prisoner. Instead, share in suffering for the gospel, relying on the power of God. He has saved us and called us with a holy calling, not according to our works, but according to his own purpose and grace, which was given to us in Christ Jesus before time began.
2 Timothy 1:8–9

Question: Are there areas in your communication with your husband where you can say, *Yes! I've got this nailed!* Another question, are there ways your husband knocks it out of the park when it comes to communicating with you?

God has gifted you both with unique strengths. Do you regularly recognize and acknowledge your husband's strengths? Take a moment to make a mental list of all the reasons why you love your husband. How is he a gift from God? How has he blessed you and your family? How has he grown in character and godliness while you've known him? Recognizing good traits in your husband has a way of communicating your admiration and devotion to him.

What about weaknesses in communication? When a hard topic comes up, such as finances, sex, or priorities, how do you and your husband handle it? What are your default tendencies? Does one of you take the lead and run the other one over? Or do you sit and complain about how you don't want to deal with it and wish you didn't have to? Maybe you flat out ignore hard conversations because they are just...too...hard.

We all have tendencies we either struggle with or thrive within. The task in this chapter is to discern a) What are your mutual communication ruts and tendencies? b) How do you discuss them without becoming offended? And c) How can you begin combating them together?

LET ME COUNT THE WAYS…

I am so grateful for how quickly Ryan can clearly help me resolve relational conflict with others. He's *always* been strong at mediating conflicts. He's like a bomb defuser in a Bruce Willis movie: calm, collected, and precise. Me, however, that's a different story. If you've ever seen the movie *Inside Out*, then you will be familiar with the character, *Anger*. My emotions tend to run hot during relational conflict because I take it personally. Given enough time, I start to boil over and soon my bomb-handling husband is at work defusing me!

Still, Ryan has his struggles, too. Part of the reason he's so cool in hot situations is because he's a compartmentalizer. He has no problem cordoning off areas of his heart if they're too difficult or intense to handle. This means he can go for extended periods of time with unresolved internal conflict. He's even told me he sometimes operates with an underlying angst and he's not sure what's wrong. He'll act fine, but I can tell something is amiss. Thankfully I've been able to help him by learning to ask questions that get beneath the surface and provide him opportunities to open up.

If you've been married for a while, you're likely as familiar with your husband's communication strengths and weaknesses as you are your own. This level of familiarity only comes over time and by making mistakes—hopefully with more than a few successes along the way. Not all tendencies are bad, and if our experience is any indication, your communication tendencies might have upsides if you're willing to work together.

RECOGNIZE AND OWN YOUR TENDENCIES

Again, I ask the question, how do you *tend* to respond when it comes to communicating through hard conversations? Are you good with words or do you stumble through? Why? What about the underlying general irritation? Ryan can sense when I am trying to hide my irritation, especially when it comes to him doing certain household chores a different way than I do them. Where in your marriage are your tendencies not edifying to your husband and why?

For a long time I blamed my weaknesses on my past. I felt like my parents weren't great at communicating through conflict, so neither was I. Although it might be partly true, it was more of a crutch and excuse than it was a starting point for my sanctification.

Do you see the pride in this? When you don't own your weaknesses then you'll never have a place to begin. Shifting responsibility from yourself keeps you on the merry-go-round of dysfunction. Remember that God has given you a spirit of love, power, and a sound mind to help you get off this crazy ride and grow into the person he is calling you to become. Own and recognize your tendencies. Bring them to the feet of Jesus and petition his counsel.

HUMBLY DISCUSS WEAKNESSES (YOURS AND HIS)

Humility and honesty go a long way when it comes to talking about each other's communication ruts. As I've learned, there is a way to have this conversation without being self-deprecating or prideful. Take time to set the stage and head into this conversation prayerfully. Be ready to feel offended, but more importantly, be ready for growth and maturity. Honest conversations will produce fruitful results.

In John 15:1–2, Jesus reminds us that he is the vine, and we are the branches. We must abide in him. Aside from Christ and his work within us we cannot produce fruit, and whatever parts of us that do produce fruit will be pruned to produce better, healthier fruit. Remember this when you sit down with your husband to discuss areas where you can improve your communication. Pruning is a must for those already producing fruit. In fact, I'd argue that you're already producing fruit by the very fact that you decided to have a conversation!

A few tangible steps as you begin:

Sit, hold hands, and pray together. Ask the Lord for soft and open hearts toward one another. Bring your Bible. Bring pen and paper to take notes. Toss your phone in a drawer. Get a sitter for your kids. Come humbly. Don't try to discuss every single communication tendency or weakness in one night, one or two is plenty. Doing the work like the above is a testimony to Christ's love and power at work in your marriage. So, take heart, and remember, talking about your ruts is not the objective, learning to love one another through the process is.

> ### KEY TAKEAWAY
> Identifying your sinful communication tendencies will help you combat them. We combat them through repentance; owning them, recognizing them, and discovering new ways to replace them.

MEDIOCRITY VS. MASTERY

Mediocrity	*Mastery*
Focuses on her husband's shortcomings in how he speaks to her	Acknowledges her husband's communication strengths and encourages him in them
Gets defensive when her words, tone, or timing of a conversation is called into question	Takes responsibility for her weak or lazy communication tendencies and sees them as opportunities for growth
Would rather ignore hard conversations than have them	Is unafraid to discuss hard topics in marriage because she is anchored in Christ

APPLICATION QUESTIONS

What are three ways your husband excels in his communication with you?

In what area you would like to improve in how you communicate with your husband?

Set aside time to have an honest conversation about your communication tendencies. Write down a few thoughts here after the conversation.

CHAPTER FIFTEEN

Hearing Everything He Never Said

If I speak in the tongues of men and of angels, but have not love, I am a noisy gong or a clanging cymbal.
1 Corinthians 13:1

Ryan didn't actually say, "Your lazy cooking is terrible, and it makes me feel unloved," but still, it's what I heard.

Who does he think he is? I thought. After seventeen years of marriage, I could not believe my husband was telling me he didn't feel loved because I didn't have a plan for dinner that evening. *Does he even care about the type of day I've had?*

What I wanted to say to him (and did) was, "I'm sorry, but didn't I just birth our third baby eight months ago, all the while home educating our other children, podcasting, writing books, and managing the daily chores of life in the Frederick household? And you're telling me you don't feel cared for or considered?"

Remember, my reaction was based on what I *heard*, not what he said. For the record, neither of us remembers his actual words. I do recall it was a pivotal moment in our marriage in which we were re-establishing dinnertime as a centerpiece in our daily rhythms rather than an afterthought. In fact, it's a glad burden we both share. In the past when I've been pregnant or when the kids were little, he'd often plan and prepare dinner more often than I would!

Why? Why did I hear what he didn't say, but was sort of saying, but not actually saying? Because no matter how long you've been married or how unified you are, communication with your spouse is challenging.

Ryan and I have been best friends since we were seventeen years old, and we *still* have breakdowns in our communication. We have grown in our skills and ability to handle communication dysfunction, but we still have issues. Praise God for not leaving us disconnected in our dysfunction!

Let's look at what led us to this communication breakdown.

WHOSE FAULT WAS IT?

Ours. We were both at fault. His timing and tone could have been better (he admits to this). Obviously, my response could have been better, but back then it felt impossible to respond patiently.

I couldn't hear what he was saying because I interpreted this conversation as being an indictment against me and a reminder of all my failures. Not just a failure to hear what he was really saying, but failure in areas of our life in which I strive to succeed, things like loving and serving my family in our home through meals and discipleship. What else could he have been doing but attacking me, right? Wrong.

When Ryan tactfully asked if I could start looking at some new recipes, or trying a new dish here and there, he was doomed from the start. Again, he wasn't attacking my current efforts; he was attempting to help us re-establish another level of order and bring back some of the things we love and value.

Life was hectic with an eight-month old and two other young kiddos, plus writing, cooking, home management, home education, and trying to be a good wife…you can see where this is going (I'll bet your schedule is full too). Ryan's timing may have not been the best, but his request to make a thoughtful meal was not unreasonable. After all, timing and tone are huge factors in healthy communication (covered later), but the issue here had more to do with how I felt and *why*.

FEELINGS V. REALITY

Ultimately, it was my pride that was hurt because I thought Ryan was questioning my love and devotion to our family while pointing out my failures in the process. But eventually I realized he was merely sharing new ideas that might help me achieve one of the goals we had articulated that year: loving our family (and others) through meals.

Fast forward to today, years after our "what's for dinner" fight, and you'll find me *happily* prepping the week's meals every Sunday. (Well, *almost* every Sunday.) Through our conflict, we grew. On the other side of it, I found a deep well of joy that spurs and encourages me to love and honor my family—specifically Ryan, in this tangible way.

SAVED BY SALVATION

If you listen to the Fierce Marriage podcast then you probably hear us say this all the time, but it's the truth, and I'll say it again: We would not be here today, doing what we do, if it weren't for the gospel: the Good News of Jesus Christ saving us from the eternal death we deserve outside of his grace!

Instead of storming off in anger or giving each other the cold shoulder—grabbing our phones to scroll and ignoring the elephant in the room—God has given us a *better* way to communicate. The way of love. It is a Fruit of the Spirit (Galatians 5:22–23) and is clearly defined in 1 Corinthians 13:1–8,

> *If I speak in the tongues of men and of angels, but have not love, I am a noisy gong or a clanging cymbal. And if I have prophetic powers, and understand all mysteries and all knowledge, and if I have all faith, so as to remove mountains, but have not love, I am nothing. If I give away all I have, and if I deliver up my body to be burned, but have not love, I gain nothing. Love is patient and kind; love does not envy or boast; it is not arrogant or rude. It does not insist on its own way; it is not irritable or resentful; it does not rejoice at wrongdoing, but rejoices with the truth. Love bears all things, believes all things, hopes all things, endures all things. Love never ends. As for prophecies, they will pass away; as for tongues, they will cease; as for knowledge, it will pass away.*

If we don't take the time to understand the blessing of communication and develop the skills needed to communicate (speak and act) clearly and lovingly to our spouse, how can we expect to have a God-honoring marriage?

EMOTIONS ARE NOT THE ENEMY

There are no shortcuts to learning how to communicate well with your spouse. It takes time and energy to filter through your emotions and to be reminded that you're on the same team!

Emotions are not the enemy. God created us with emotions to be able to express love, appreciation, or frustration. But if we elevate our emotions above God's Word and authority, then we have an idolatry issue. We can't let them run loose like a wild horse; they need to be reined in.[12]

This tends to be the struggle with wives when it comes to communicating with their husbands. Everything is good until it's not...either he says something (or doesn't say something when *we* thought he should've said something) and our pride, insecurities, fears, and anger flare up, and suddenly we can't string together two words to ask for clarity.

Instead of feeling like we are on a team, we feel attacked and do what anyone being attacked would do: we protect ourselves and strategize our responses, attack back, and / or retreat.

How do you begin to love your spouse when you *feel* attacked? Where do you get the strength and patience to stick around when you would rather retreat?

Humility is the key. There are several ways in which we can communicate with our spouse, but it must be done with a heart and attitude of humility. Humility that flows out of the recognition that we are *both sinners,* made in God's image, equal recipients of his grace. As a follower of Christ and wife to my husband, I am

---

12. Rachel Jancovik, *Loving the Little Years, Motherhood in the Trenches* (Moscow, ID: Canon Press, 2010).

now charged with the responsibility to love and cherish him, even and especially in how I speak to him *and* in how I hear him.

> **KEY TAKEAWAY**
> It's *very* possible to hear things incorrectly. A wise wife seeks clarity before accusing her husband and responding out of anger.

MEDIOCRITY VS. MASTERY

Mediocrity	*Mastery*
Only considers how *she* is affected by the conversation	Stops to consider how her response may be mistaken
Quick to blame her husband and slow to admit fault of her own	Slow to blame and willing to admit it when wrong
Believes feelings are reality	Knows that feelings are not reality

APPLICATION QUESTIONS

Think of a time or two when you mistakenly took your husband's words as an attack. How could you have responded differently in those moments? (This question and the next one assume your husband was not being malicious.)

Why do you think you felt attacked in that moment?

What are three clarifying questions you have ready for the next time you feel attacked?

CHAPTER SIXTEEN

Consuming and Being Consumed

Let the word of Christ dwell in you richly, teaching and admonishing one another in all wisdom, singing psalms and hymns and spiritual songs, with thankfulness in your hearts to God. And whatever you do, in word or deed, do everything in the name of the Lord Jesus, giving thanks to God the Father through him.
Colossians 3:16–17

We have a large apple tree on the side of our property and it's one of my favorite trees. In late summer I find our kiddos climbing it with their friends, foraging for a ripe apple or two. Our youngest daughter will consume an entire sour green apple with a half-hearted smile because she is too prideful to admit she doesn't want to eat the fruit she picked. She knows, this isn't how apples are supposed to taste, but still, she forces it down.

Though I love this tree, we've yet to fully enjoy its fruit. The first summer we lived in our home, we had a record-setting heat wave that blasted all the fruit, causing the apples to fall before they had ripened. The following year, there was a caterpillar's nest on the backside that we didn't catch until our neighbor alerted us. The pests ravaged our crop, burrowing through hundreds of budding apples and making the larger ones brown before they dropped. Our big, beautiful apple tree hasn't been producing well, but neither we nor the previous property owners helped it much either.

The family who owned our house before us let the tree grow wild, never pruning it or tending to its branches. As new owners of land larger than a front yard, we found ourselves quickly overwhelmed by the workload. So, we never took the time to read up on pests and pruning and other peculiarities of cultivating fruitful mini orchards. We did nothing to augment the nutrients in the soil or ensure harmful fungi didn't sicken their roots. While we were hopeful the trees would produce on their own, we were sadly unsurprised when our crop quality was subpar.

Communication in your marriage is like that apple tree. While it can bear fruit on its own, the fruit won't be at its best until you tend to the tree's health. Have you done the work needed to produce ripe, delicious apples? Have you taken measures to guard against scorching, pests, and pestilence? Have you fertilized the soil around your tree's root system? Or are you like us, naively but hopefully sitting back, watching and waiting to enjoy ripe, delicious fruit with minimal effort?

Maybe it's time to prune some branches, spray your leaves, and tend to your soil. What sorts of negative communication growth is hindering your fruitfulness? What undercurrents of unspoken frustration, bitterness, or pride could be poisoning your soil? And what pests of distraction, negativity, and time-consumption are killing your fruit on the vine?

This is a charge to take inventory on what your mind consumes and your heart dwells on daily. Are there shows, music, or social media apps and sites you need to prune from your life? Maybe there is a podcast or two that needs to be axed from your daily rotation. Or could there be latent unforgiveness for your husband, a family member, or a friend who has encapsulated your heart in hardened scales and made you impervious to correction?

Whatever it is, we can know for certain what kind of communication tree we are growing by the sorts of communication fruit it bears. If we're ever to turn spoiled fruit into a bountiful communication crop, we must look at what we consume as well as what most consumes us.

CONSUMING AND BEING CONSUMED

This may go without saying, but the content you allow into your heart, mind, and soul matters. It all contributes to the fruit you bear. This is true from the food you eat to how you spend your time. The quality and quantity of your consumption will produce something in your life. Whether it's healthy or unhealthy, godly, or sinful, depends on what you allow in and the rate at which it is consumed.

For example, if I am watching shows or getting lost on social media rabbit holes where wives degrade their husbands or speak in a manner that cheapens marriage, I need to discern and ask myself, *How is this affecting my view of my marriage and my husband? And how will this affect my communication with him?* Don't kid yourself. If you start devaluing your man—knowingly or not—it will affect how you communicate with him.

Maybe you desire to *feel* closer to your husband and aren't sure why the disconnect feels annoyingly consistent. It's time to reevaluate. What are you consuming? What consumes you? What are the themes and messages circling inside your head? Do you routinely feel angry, afraid, discontent, or ungrateful? Clearly these are not ideas from God. He desires unity for your marriage and Spirit-fueled fruit bearing in your communication with your husband. (Galatians 5:22–23)

FROM CONSUMING TO BEING CONSUMED

We've looked at how what we consume affects the fruit we bear, but perhaps what matters most is what, or Who, consumes us. The author of Hebrews reminds us that "our God is a consuming fire" (Hebrews 12:29). In context, that phrase refers to our God who commands reverent awe and obedience from all mankind. But most peculiarly, the verses that immediately follow the recognition that God is a consuming fire describe the kindness, hospitality, righteousness, and confidence of those who follow Christ. The realization of God's majesty forever changes how we view and treat others, and this is often most evident in how we speak to our husbands.

Are you consumed by and with our marvelous God? Does he consume your heart, your mind, and your soul? Do you visit the throne room of grace? (Hebrews 4:16) Most practically, does God's word consume and govern your heart? The Bible is not simply a resource for knowledge about God. The woman of God reads her Bible to *know* her Savior so that her affections for him might overwhelm her in such a way that they are undeniably present in her speech and actions, beginning with her husband.

The more you are consumed by Christ, the more you desire what he desires. His eternal promises and treasures become the good fruit you hunger to consume. His joy becomes your strength for the days ahead and your words will reflect his all-consuming presence in your life.

> **KEY TAKEAWAY**
>
> What you habitually consume determines the communication fruit you bear.

MEDIOCRITY VS. MASTERY

Mediocrity	*Mastery*
Is apathetic toward the work needed to produce good communication fruit	Faithfully puts in the work, trusting God's faithfulness to produce the fruit
Doesn't mitigate what she consumes and is unaware of its effects	Carefully watches what she allows to enter her heart and mind
Is consumed by self and desires instead of the things of God	Consumed and by God and seeks to obey him

APPLICATION QUESTIONS

What does it mean to "Let the word of Christ dwell in you richly"? Reread Colossians 3:16–17 if needed.

How might letting the word of Christ dwelling in you change the communication fruit you're bearing in your marriage?

Are there any areas of your speech, thought life, tone, or attitudes that need pruning? If so, which?

CHAPTER SEVENTEEN

Salty and Sweet, Oh What a Treat!

*Do not be overcome by evil,
but overcome evil with good.*
Romans 12:21

A running joke in our marriage is how Ryan considers me the "salty" one. If you've heard any of our podcast episodes then you may have heard Ryan say, "This episode is brought to you by Selena's Secret Sauce. Salty and Sweet, oh what a treat!" or something like that. No such sauce exists yet, but I wouldn't put it past my husband to develop some sort of savory and sweet concoction and smack a carefully designed label on it and give me the first bottle as a gag gift. We shall see.

To be transparent, I'm not sure I like being called "salty" because of what the word implies. It makes me think of an angry pirate who is tougher than nails, has "seen some things," and has more curses and filth coming out of his mouth than anything else. I don't think Ryan is inferring that I am any of those things, but admittedly, I did have a "saltier" chapter in my past marked by sinful anger in my heart.

Naturally, the anger in my heart overflowed into how I spoke to my husband. In our earlier years of marriage it felt safer to me to put up a tough front with Ryan instead of sharing what was going on inside my heart. When I did share whatever it was that I was dealing with, my language was typically littered with unbecoming diction and laced with anger. I take full responsibility for my words and have repented and found forgiveness for that season of life. However I should note that the battle was twofold.

By nature Ryan is competitive. So, naturally it follows that his communication was, and continues to this day to be, intentional and strategic. I would say it's a strength, but it's taken time for him to learn how to wield it as a tool to reconcile rather than a weapon to win. All too often this led to him not truly hearing my heart. He'd technically win the bout, but we would be further away from each other than we were when we started. I'm happy to say that he talks at length about this in his corresponding book, titled *How a Husband Speaks*.

We are wired differently and that's a blessing, but we still needed to figure out how to use our differences to our advantage. As a young bride, I would try to deal with tough marital issues at first, but over time I'd get tired of losing. My frustration would lead to two ways of handling the subsequent arguments. I would disengage from the conversation since resignation seemed simpler, or I would fly off the handle and let my salty side show. We both needed to grow. Resigning wasn't an option, nor could I let loose because the release felt good.

One of the most beautiful aspects of marriage is that you're forced to face your failures (covenant means you're bound together) and you have a safe place to do so (your covenant is governed by Christ-like love). After much trial and error, we began to realize how God was calling us to become better communicators.

Ryan needed to grow by learning how to be a husband who leads and loves through tender, patient, and emotionally intelligent communication. For me, I was a wife who needed to submit her salty side to the Lord and learn to trust that her husband would see her as his wife and not an opponent to be defeated. It's a tricky place to be. You could call it the married-people Mexican standoff, where you both need to de-escalate the situation, but you're also both wondering who of you will surrender first. Someone needs to trust the other for anyone to survive. Ideally, you take the first step together.

WORDS BY THOSE CREATED *IN* AND CONFORMED *TO* GOD'S IMAGE

As the Lord continued to draw us unto himself through our various communication dysfunctions, we were reminded of the fact that we are his image bearers (Genesis 1:27) who are called to be "conformed to the image of his Son" (Romans 8:29).

So, we began to ask ourselves, *Do our actions toward each other clearly reflect the image of God's Son?* And, *Are we speaking words to each other that are becoming of those who bear God's image?* I discovered how my words left deep wounds in my husband's heart, and he learned how his words only hardened mine. Our words began to soften, and our defenses started to lower. How could the same mouths that speak to each other like this during the week also be used to worship and bless the Lord on Sunday mornings?

Ouch. That last conviction hurt the most, because James seemed to be speaking directly to us, "from the same mouth come both blessing and cursing. My brethren, these things ought not to be this way. Does a fountain send out from the same opening both fresh and bitter water?" (James 3:10–11)

Thank God for his timely and everlasting work of sanctification, especially in the ways we speak to each other in marriage. I'll let Ryan divulge the details of God's work in his heart in his own book. For me, I was most clearly reminded of just how powerful my words are as a woman and especially as a wife. I'd like to share those reminders with you.

A wife's words hold immense weight in her husband's heart and should be used as a tool for building him up and not as a weapon to tear him down (Ephesians 4:29). They should be used to bring life and not death (Proverbs 18:21), to bless and not to curse (Romans 12:14). By his words, God created, and by our words, we reveal the true depths of our hearts (Luke 6:45). Perhaps most startlingly, every wife will give an account for the careless words she speaks (Matthew 12:36). The list could continue, but how much more evidence do we need to be convinced: our words are powerful! This should sober us as well as motivate us to use them wisely and skillfully in our marriage.

DON'T POLLUTE YOUR DIRECT LINE

Your words matter, and as a wife you have a direct line to your husband's heart. We must be careful not to pollute it. If you have been married for any amount of time you know the power you wield with your words. No one else's words hold the same weight to him as yours do. Therefore we must be so careful to use words with accuracy. We must say what we mean to say and be disciplined enough to withhold words that might feel good to say but mean something other than what we mean.

Remember back to the last heated argument you had with your husband. Did you say exactly what you meant to say? What you say affects him, and perhaps in ways you don't know. As I learned with my husband, he feels the full weight of *all* my words even in the moments when I'm being flippant and don't intend their full meaning. He feels each word deeply because he cares more about what I say than anyone else. He's not being sensitive; he's just taking my words for what they mean. Like I said, it's sobering.

My angry rants early on in our marriage didn't get us anywhere, and despite how I thought they'd work, they never helped me feel better either. Instead, they made me feel worse and they proved to be obstacles keeping us from reconciling. Word vomiting only polluted the direct line I had to Ryan's heart.

By my coarse or careless words, I chipped away at his trust because his distrust in my words led to a distrust in my actions. For example, there was a season when I'd offer to do something nice as a way of making up with him, but instead of first reconciling through communication, I'd just do whatever it was. *Actions speak louder*, right? Well, apparently that only works if the actions and the words align. I'd extend an olive branch with a meal or some married-style advances in bed, but I'd immediately sense his hesitation. After some time and tension, he'd articulate that in that moment he was struggling to trust my words, intentions, and actions. To him, it felt like I was simply reacting to his frustration because of my angry rant.

The problem was that he was partially right. I wanted to make it up to him, but first I needed to clean out the polluted line by owning my part in it. Over time, I came to realize that I couldn't make it up to him without owning my behavior and the angry, damaging words I spoke. It was the only way we could move forward and build trust. My anger needed to be brought under control. Otherwise he couldn't trust my actions because they would only be a manipulation tactic forcing him to get over how he felt.

You can't pollute the line to your husband's heart and move on. Take the time to stop and clean out the line by owning your sin and repenting. Only then can you move toward godly communication. For now, let's look closely at what the Bible says about anger.

THE BIBLE AND ANGER

God's Word is chock full of warnings about fits of rage and unbridled anger. Anger itself is not a sin, but your heart motivation and how you act because of your anger is where it gets dangerous. Biblically speaking, you can handle your anger toward your husband in a few ways.

Overcome Evil with Good

There are many occasions where anger is a valid response. There may be moments in your marriage when your husband says or does something to sin against you. For example, imagine your husband getting home after a bad day at work, and instead of lovingly greeting you by kiss or word, he throws his keys on the counter, storms through the house, and speaks critically toward you and impatiently toward the kids. No kiss, no sweet "Hello honey," no "How was your day?" Nothing. You, on the other hand, have had a tough day too. And, despite your tough day, you're excited to see your man! I may be exaggerating, but in this and instances like it, there's no doubt you'll feel some sort of frustration or anger.

So, what do you do?

You can respond with a harsh word and stir up anger (Proverbs 15:1) in yourself and in your husband. (It's not a great option, but it's an option nonetheless). Or you can do something else to overcome evil with good (Romans 12:21) in the spirit of being at peace with all men (Romans 12:18). Does this mean you enable your husband's sin? Not at all. It does mean you choose a better time to address it. For now, you seek ways to de-escalate the tension and speak in ways that encourage, disarm, and draw out the best in your husband. Ideally, he'd do the same for you.

Love your Enemy

Your husband is not your enemy, but there are times when his actions sure feel like enemy attacks. How do we deal with moments when we have "enemy feelings" as a result? By loving him. "But I say to you, love your enemies and pray for those who persecute you, so that you may be sons of your Father who is in heaven. For he makes the sun rise on the evil and on the good and sends rain on the just and on the unjust" (Matthew 5:43–45).

Following that, Jesus said, "For if you love those who love you, what reward do you have? Do not even the tax collectors do the same?" (Matthew 5:46) Remember, he is your husband and you're still on the same team, even if it doesn't feel like it at times. Love him like your partner even when he's acting like the opposition. Doing so is evidence of taking Jesus at his word.

Quickly Listen; Slowly Speak

James' command is timely here, "Know this, my loved brothers: let every person be quick to hear, slow to speak, slow to anger; for the anger of man does not produce the righteousness of God"

(James 1:19–20). I'm always amazed at how disarming a genuine, apt question can be. Instead of reacting in anger, be curious. Why is your husband so riled up? What's happening in his heart? What sorts of obstacles did he face throughout his day? Ask questions and listen intently. Try not to respond immediately, but listen and consider with genuine curiosity. Your anger will not—it cannot—produce the righteousness of God. You know what can? The fruits of the Spirit. So, instead of choosing anger, choose those. Doing so is evidence of having "crucified the flesh with its passions and desires" (Galatians 5:26).

Be the Right Amount of Salty

Jesus calls his disciples to be the right kind of salty. Whereas my saltiness was based on anger, Christ's saltiness is based on obedience. In talking about sharing his message, Jesus said, "You are the salt of the earth, but if salt has lost its taste, how shall its saltiness be restored? It is no longer good for anything except to be thrown out and trampled under people's feet." Jesus has called all his disciples to be preachers of the gospel, and as wives, we can often forget it applies even to how we speak to our husbands in the home. In moments when you'd like to respond to your husband with anger (and even if it's justified), remind him instead of the gospel. Tactfully show him the kindness of Christ and enliven his heart to the promises of God. Though it's not a guarantee he will immediately snap out of his current emotion, it is a guarantee of your obedience to Christ.

Wield your words well, sister in Christ. You have a direct and exclusive line to your husband's heart. Use your words as God-given tools to glorify Him and to edify your husband. Doing so ensures you'll be a salty wife in the best sort of way.

> **KEY TAKEAWAY**
>
> A wife's words hold immense weight in her husband's ears; choose them wisely.

MEDIOCRITY VS. MASTERY

Mediocrity	*Mastery*
Often careless with her words	Understands the weight of her words and selects them carefully
Gives way to angry rants	Exercises self-control when an angry rant *feels* better
Habitually slow to listen and quick to speak	Is slow to speak and quick to listen

APPLICATION QUESTIONS

As a wife, you have a direct line to the deepest parts of your husband's heart. What are a few potential ways you have polluted or misused your direct line, either knowingly or unknowingly?

What are two to three specific ways you can intend to use your direct line to bless your husband in the coming days and weeks?

CHAPTER EIGHTEEN

A Soft Answer Turns Away Wrath

*A soft answer turns away wrath,
but a harsh word stirs up anger.*
Proverbs 15:1

Experience has taught me that certain seasons of life feel like they're made up of time-to-get-out-the-door transitional moments. They are never perfect and often require all my patience and gumption to choose joy.

Every time our family rushes out the door to catch a flight or hit the road for a long road trip, we always do it patiently, perfectly, graciously, and on time. I'm sure it's the same for you, and now we both know I'm being completely tongue-in-cheek. On these hectic days—right as I holler, "We need to leave in twenty minutes!"—our car is usually not packed, children have spilled breakfast on their clean clothes, and Ryan decides he is going to head upstairs to take a shower "real quick." Lord help me.

Sidenote, Ryan has *always* liked to take showers right before we leave to go anywhere, which drives me crazy (he knows this) because it always puts us right at, or a little beyond the scheduled departure time. He would argue that we have never missed a flight or scheduled vacation because of this (and he's right—sigh). Regardless, by this time my patience is always running thin.

As my familiar anger bubbles up, I try to take a few deep breaths and remind myself that we *will* make it on ti—

"Are you seriously going to go take a shower right now?!" Too late. "We haven't loaded the car!" "I haven't even gotten dressed!" The kids are…" (I'm sure you can fill in the blank).

I feel hopeless in these situations because no matter how hard I try to prepare for a smooth, happy departure, it never works. Instead, we usually leave the house in a tizzy, the kids arguing, and we question whether the trip is even worth the effort and heartache.

I try my best to avoid these situations by tending to the details. I used to believe that if I could anticipate and prepare, then I could avoid any heartache or frustration. I still find myself gravitating toward this flawed belief. And when I do, boy, am I wrong.

Granted, every day was not meant to be care-free, when I can kick back on the couch, sip chamomile tea, and bask in the glories of domesticity. The life of a Christian woman is too laced with eternal purpose to be free of responsibility. However, I can kick back and reflect (and experience freedom) for other reasons, like remembering how good Jesus still is in the middle of my chaos and despite my imperfections. I can remember how he's the one who speaks to literal storms, and they obey. This isn't an excuse or some fresh "bless this mess" truism to make women feel better while accepting dysfunction in the home, but rather an acknowledgment of our humanity, and more importantly, Christ's divinity.

CAN I LEARN SOME PATIENCE ALREADY?

Oh how impatiently we hope to learn patience! But that's precisely the point, isn't it? Learning patience is like waiting for sourdough to rise; rushing only ruins it. True patience is learned when you least want to learn it, and if I'm waiting for an easy or convenient time to learn how to respond softly, patiently, and with kindness to my husband during difficult, stressful seasons, it will never come. Why? Because patience requires resistance. It's not weight training without the weight, so how can we expect to grow stronger if we never grab the next dumbbell size up?

Yes, we can do our best to see the signs and eliminate physical factors like hunger and tiredness (covered in the previous chapter) but we cannot anticipate or control every situation to make it easier for us to respond well. So, it's in those moments when our trust in God's Word is truly put to the test. That's the weight. You can either lift it and grow, or you can cast it aside and do whatever it is you've always done. You may not like it (especially in the moment), but you must choose.

This is the precise point when the temperature rises and the dross is burned away (Proverbs 25:4). No matter how you feel, whatever the surrounding circumstances, regardless of the marital dynamics, and despite the chaos of the home, God's Word is *always* instructive. And here's what it says about how we respond, arguably and especially when stressful situations present themselves: "A soft answer turns away wrath, but a harsh word stirs up anger" (Proverbs 15:1).

It doesn't get any clearer than that. God still leaves you with a choice: you can either respond to your husband softly, which I take to include kindness, patience, and respect. Or you can respond harshly, in which case you mustn't be surprised when the conflict escalates and tensions rise.

Sounds easy right? That depends on how you define *easy*. I do know you're not alone.

To revisit a point I made earlier, I think we take for granted just how active the Holy Spirit is in moments like these! He is actively at work producing fruit in you, especially in moments when extra patience is required. It's then that he begins to produce fruit of love, joy, peace, patience, kindness, goodness, faithfulness, gentleness, and self-control—everything you need to give a soft answer. And a soft answer well-timed will disarm your husband's anger and begin to soften his heart.

In the moments when you would rather speak harshly to him, remember that God has given you the patience and self-control to "softly" answer your husband when it isn't easy or desirable to do so.

YOU CAN'T DO THIS ON YOUR OWN STRENGTH

It will feel impossible to do this on your own because you cannot conjure up enough self-control or patience by your own efforts. You and I need our Lord's help. We need to know him through communing with him daily. Only by sitting at the feet of our Father will you begin to see the effects of his love on your soul. Through him you will see the Fruit of his Spirit begin to grow in you, transforming and enabling you to respond gently.

When I try to respond by my own strength, I fail. I've learned the hard way that when I get riled up and spew angry words at my husband and children about being late and unprepared, it doesn't leave room for the Holy Spirit to produce the fruit in my heart that he desires. Nor is it edifying to my family.

But God.

God is so good to provide us with what I like to call "practice opportunities" throughout the day. No doubt there will be another opportunity for you to choose to respond softly to your husband. Will you choose softness or harshness? Honey or vinegar? Salty or sweet?

Choosing to love as Christ loved by responding to your husband lovingly will get easier and more desirable the more you do it. When you choose to respond to your husband how Christ would respond, you not only turn away wrath, but you face down your own anger with love. This, in turn, models to your husband a love that is otherworldly, since he likely knows you're at a tipping point and he's watching to see what you will do. Then you let the love of Christ tip you toward softness and love.

It's right at that moment when God's love unfolds. When someone witnesses the active, real, tangible, and transformative love of Christ through others, it leaves a real and lasting impression. And love has a multiplying effect in the home. When you love supernaturally—especially in critical moments—don't be surprised when joy, patience, kindness, and the other fruits of the Spirit are multiplied.

Christ himself is love, and when Christ is the fount from which your love springs, everyone in the household is well-watered, especially your husband.

PRECIOUS, SLOW SANCTIFICATION

Through my many "practice opportunities" over the years, God has grown me. He's shown me how to better respond to my husband in life's panic-inducing moments. And many lessons were learned after the failure, not before. But God is gracious still. Where there is failure, grace and mercy abound. "And God is able to make all grace abound to you, so that having all sufficiency in all things at all times, you may abound in every good work" (2 Corinthians 9:8). *All* sufficiency at *all* times is exhaustive, and not just so we might eek out a good work here and there, but that we might *abound* in them. But abounding doesn't happen in an instant; it takes time and the ongoing experience of the work of Christ.

Failing, repenting, and growing is what sanctification looks like, and it's what makes difficult moments so redemptive. Christ is always at work in them and around them, and in my less-and-less rare, lucid moments of obedience, when I submit my anger and frustration to the Lord, he is always sufficient and faithful to meet me there. But when I mess up and let my saltiness show (not the good kind), I can repent to Christ, ask my husband for forgiveness, dust myself off, and grow just a little more.

> **KEY TAKEAWAY**
> Chaotic moments are ripe opportunities for soft answers. We can either recognize the opportunity and embrace it or reject it and respond out of our flesh.

MEDIOCRITY VS. MASTERY

Mediocrity	*Mastery*
Allows chaos of circumstances to dictate how she speaks	Allows God's Words to instruct hers
Responds without patience or regard for others	Combats chaos of circumstances with gentle and patient responses
Permits anger and frustration to fester	Quick to repent upon failure to respond in a godly manner

APPLICATION QUESTIONS

In terms of your communication, how have you handled chaos and stress with your husband? Do you get short and snappy, angry, quiet, or something else? However you respond, why do you think that's your tendency?

What passage of scripture can you commit to memory and recall during the next chaotic moment you experience? If you're looking for ideas, read back a few pages and find one that was mentioned. Feel free to write it below.

Final Words

FORTIFY, PROTECT, AND SHINE

You will fortify and protect your marriage by pursuing godly communication. Unity in conversation is not *solely* to get you through life with a happy marriage. It's a way God shines through you. Matthew 5:14–16 reads,

> *You are the light of the world. A city set on a hill cannot be hidden. Nor do people light a lamp and put it under a basket, but on a stand, and it gives light to all in the house. In the same way, let your light shine before others, so that they may see your good works and give glory to your Father who is in heaven.*

There is something good, attractive, and otherworldly about a couple who speaks to each other with great care, kindness, consideration, and love. This is especially true during the inevitable storms of life that bring conflict to a marriage.

Fortify your marriage, protect it, keep it safe from manipulative, lazy, thoughtless, or divided communication by putting Christ at the center. Remember the gospel: the Good News that Jesus came to earth, lived a perfect life, and died a sinner's death; rose again on the third day, conquering death and sin forever! He is our model for loving communication. In him we find life, truth, and the way to unity and oneness in our communication with each other.

Stay fierce,
Selena

ALSO AVAILABLE

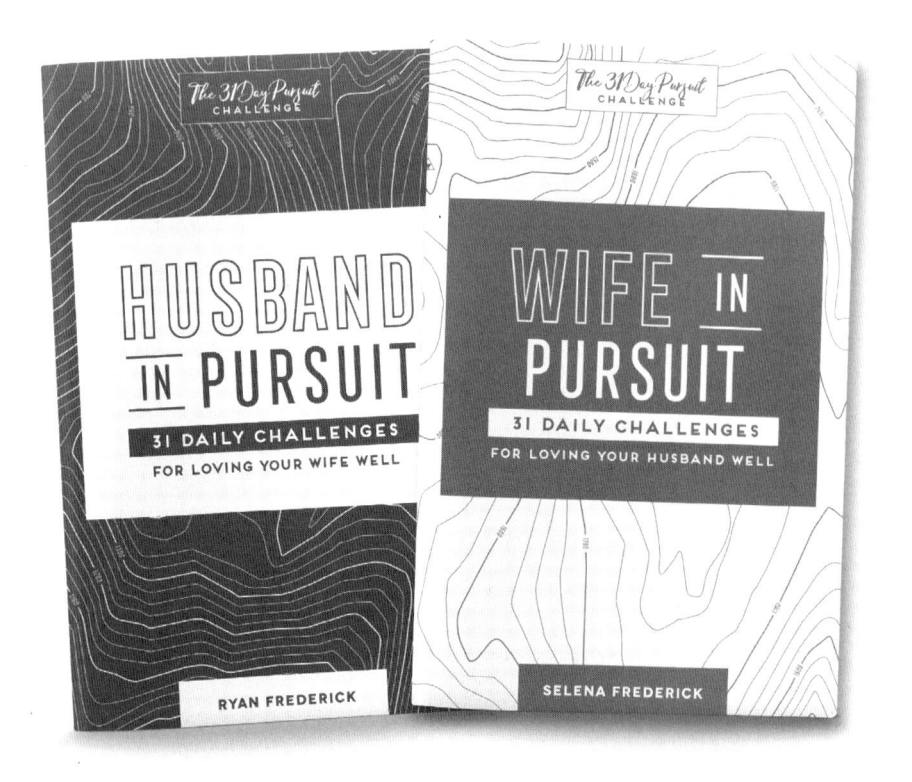

Husband in Pursuit and *Wife in Pursuit* offer a gospel-centered path for couples who want to learn to creatively love each other as Christ has loved them. Over thirty-one days, you and your husband will dive into God's Word, rediscover how Christ has pursued you, and take intentional action to pursue each other.

Take the 31-Day Pursuit Challenge together.

Learn more at 31DayPursuit.com

ALSO AVAILABLE

40 Prayers for My Wife
Drawing near to God for the woman you love.
by Ryan Frederick

40 Prayers for My Husband
Drawing near to God for the man you love.
by Selena Frederick

Prayer is your first and most powerful weapon when fighting for your marriage. What could happen if you diligently and consistently sought God's heart for your husband? How different would your marriage be?

This bundle is written to help couples learn the habit of praying for one another through the many seasons of marriage.

Learn more at 40Prayers.com

The wisest of women builds her house,
but folly with her own hands tears it down.

Proverbs 14:1